Competition Law and Policy Reviews

The Role of Guidelines in Fostering Competition Policy in Tunisia

OECD

BETTER POLICIES FOR BETTER LIVES

Please cite this publication as:
OECD (2024), *The Role of Guidelines in Fostering Competition Policy in Tunisia*, Competition Law and Policy Reviews, OECD Publishing, Paris, https://doi.org/10.1787/82f72c0e-en.

ISBN 978-92-64-63774-0 (print)
ISBN 978-92-64-65537-9 (pdf)
ISBN 978-92-64-50635-0 (HTML)
ISBN 978-92-64-35876-8 (epub)

Competition Law and Policy Reviews
ISSN 2220-7767 (print)
ISSN 2220-9158 (online)

Photo credits: Cover © AmnajKhetsamtip/Getty Images.

Corrigenda to OECD publications may be found on line at: www.oecd.org/about/publishing/corrigenda.htm.

Foreword

Competition guidelines are key advocacy instruments for competition authorities and can be especially useful in younger competition regimes, where the competition culture is still emerging and where competition agencies are often young, inexperienced and are faced with limited resources. Guidelines are documents by which an administrative authority communicates general principles, methodologies and decision-making practices, – in this case with respect to application and interpretation of various provisions of its competition law – allowing for increased transparency, predictability and legal certainty for the private sector.

Competition guidelines commonly seek to explain the law; indicate how a competition authority interprets and applies the legislative provisions; refer to any relevant case law or prior decisions, which assist the competition authority with its interpretation; and provide case or hypothetical examples.

This report provides insights into the framework conditions and current practice in terms of competition guidelines in Tunisia and sets out recommendations to help the country strengthen its competition advocacy framework. The successive implementation of these recommendations can support Tunisia's efforts to improve its enforcement framework and practice, aligning more closely with international best practices.

The document was produced within the framework of the "Fostering competition in Tunisia" project funded by the German Federal Ministry for Economic Cooperation and Development (BMZ) via the DispoFlex mechanism and supported by the *Deutsche Gesellschaft für Internationale Zusammenarbeit* (GIZ). The project builds on the OECD's previous analysis and aims at reviewing Tunisia's draft competition guidelines and supporting the Competition Council, the DGCEE and the Administrative Court through capacity building initiatives.

This publication benefitted from the support, inputs, review, comments and fruitful co-operation of the Competition Council, the Ministry of Trade and the GIZ. Our thanks go to Urs Schrade and Walid Wahabi from the RECAP team at the GIZ for the good co-operation, for providing support and contributing to the task of co-ordinating the project. We are grateful to the Ministry of Trade and to the Competition Council for their co-operation, commitment and support throughout the project. In particular, the authors are thankful to Houssem Eddine Touiti, Head of the competition and economic investigations department at the Ministry of Trade and his team, especially Nawal Khaldi and Mohamed Mnasser, Vice-President, Mohamed Cheikhrouhou, Rapporteur General and Habib Essid, Rapporteur at the Competition Council.

This report has been developed by a team led by Saïd Kechida composed of Marcelo Guimarães and Wouter Meester, all from the OECD Competition Division. Ori Schwartz, Head of the OECD Competition Division and António Gomes, Deputy-Director for Financial and Enterprise Affairs, provided valuable comments and inputs. The report was edited and prepared for publication by Erica Agostinho and Nasli Aouka, OECD Competition Division.

Table of contents

FIGURES

TABLES

Abbreviations and acronyms

BMZ	German Federal Ministry for Economic Cooperation and Development
COMESA	Common Market for Eastern and Southern Africa
GDP	Gross Domestic Product
ICN	International Competition Network
DGCEE	Department for Competition and Economic Investigations
INT	National Telecommunications Authority
EC	European Commission
ECJ	European Court of Justice
EU	European Union
GIZ	Deutsche Gesellschaft für Internationale Zusammenarbeit
MEA	Middle East and Africa
HHI	Herfindahl-Hirschmann Index
MoU	Memorandum of Understanding
PCC	Philippine Competition Commission
UNCTAD	United Nations Conference on Trade and Development

Executive summary

This report analyses the competition guidelines practice in Tunisia. It aims at analysing the current framework conditions for the adoption of guidelines as well as setting out recommendations to support the country's efforts to improve its enforcement and advocacy framework and align more closely with international best practices.

Tunisia started an ambitious programme to implement an effective competition law and policy. As highlighted in the 2022 OECD Peer Review of Competition Law and Policy, the conditions for the competition entities to thrive and to make a significant contribution to achieving competitive markets in the country are largely in place. If well implemented, competition law and policy can benefit the country's consumers and businesses, leading to increased productivity, innovation, growth and employment.

To further improve the legal and policy framework in line with well-established international best practices, this review suggests a number of improvements to the competition enforcement and advocacy frameworks, particularly by developing competition guidelines in four areas: merger control, fining methodology, leniency programme and compliance programme.

The report reviews Tunisia's draft guidelines on merger control and provides insights for the Tunisian authorities to consider when developing guidelines on fining methodology, leniency programme and compliance programme. This report applies an analysis and benchmarking of the competition guidelines framework and practice across the four areas, comparing the situation in Tunisia with observed practice in selected jurisdictions and best practice policies, as established by OECD instruments and work by the Competition Committee.

Key findings

The OECD's review has identified a number of shortcomings in Tunisia's competition law and policy, not the least of which the absence of competition guidelines. The publication of guidelines by administrative authorities is indeed not a common practice under Tunisian law.

The Tunisian competition law framework regarding merger review has a series of limitations, including a very high turnover-based notification threshold and the absence of two-phase and simplified merger control regime, as well as the lack of merger notification forms. If companies implement the transaction prior to notification and approval when it fulfils the conditions listed in the law (so-called gun jumping), they may be fined up to 10% of their turnover in Tunisia. While Tunisian rules related to gun jumping seem to be in line with international best practices, the absence of enforcement deviates from the international practices. Tunisian competition authorities have never sanctioned companies for gun jumping, even though non-notified transactions that fulfilled notification thresholds were identified.

The Tunisian competition law framework regarding fines for anti-competitive practices is overall in line with international standards. However, there is no established fining methodology. In many infringement decisions no pecuniary sanctions are applied. While this used to be more common in the past, there are still some cases where no fines have been imposed. This significantly reduces deterrence effects, also contributing for low incentives for infringers to use leniency applications.

The Tunisian competition law follows international standards regarding leniency programmes, but despite being in place for over 20 years, no application has ever been submitted to date. For leniency programmes to work, there must be a high risk of detection and significant sanctions, which does not seem the case in Tunisia. Anti-cartel enforcement in Tunisia is still low, and some cartel decisions were handed without a fine being imposed, significantly reducing their deterrent effect.

Competition compliance programmes are not common in Tunisia, regardless of the size of the firm. The limited enforcement, the absence of guidelines and the lack of clear roles and tasks allocation between the DGCEE and the Competition Council when it comes to competition advocacy do not facilitate the promotion and adoption of compliance programmes by Tunisian firms.

Key recommendations

To further improve the competition policy framework in line with well-established international best practices, this review suggests a number of improvements to the competition guidelines practice.

A draft document of merger guidelines was already prepared by the Tunisian competition authorities, which suggests that this should continue to be their focus in the short-term. Guidelines on fining methodology should be prioritised in a second stage, followed by guidelines on leniency and compliance programmes.

Merger control

The current draft merger control guidelines should consider addressing the following elements before being submitted to stakeholder consultation:

- In the absence of the implementation of the Peer Review recommendation to transfer responsibility for merger control to the Competition Council, ensure a more co-ordinated approach on the assessment of mergers between the Competition Council and the DGCEE.
- Specify how the competition assessment varies according to the nature of the transaction (i.e. horizontal or non-horizontal mergers).
- Provide further elements regarding market definition, which is particularly relevant since one of the notification thresholds is based on a market share test.
- Elaborate on the nature of the relevant economic test used for assessing mergers, in order to ensure a consistent and transparent review of transactions.
- Further detail how remedies should be set, including with more descriptive examples.
- Establish “safe harbours” to specify the cases that are not likely to raise competition concerns, possibly subject to a simplified procedure.
- Include additional examples and reference to relevant caselaw, providing more details on the substantive analysis and procedures of these cases.
- Introduce a glossary with explanations of relevant terminology.

Fining methodology

Developing fining methodology can help Tunisian competition authorities ensure a consistent fining policy. When developing fining guidelines, the following elements should be taken into account:

- Clearly indicate the objectives of fines.

- Spell out the methodology for setting fines, including the determination of the basic amount, its adjustment according to aggravating and mitigating circumstances and statutory limits of fines.
- Consider the gravity and duration of the infringement when setting fines.
- Whether the firm's inability to pay can be taken into account and, if so, how.

Leniency programme

The issuance of guidelines can be useful in further promoting Tunisian leniency programme. In this context, the following elements should be considered in future leniency guidelines:

- Indicate the violations covered by the leniency programme.
- Establish the eligibility criteria and the conditions to apply for leniency.
- Clearly state the benefits from the leniency programme.
- Spell out the procedural aspects of a leniency application, including who is the point of contact in the competition authority that interested parties should approach to submit an application, the possibility to request a marker and the information and evidence that should be presented.
- Explain how and to what extent confidentiality of leniency applications is ensured.
- State the consequences of leniency for civil liability.
- Provide a checklist regarding the elements that must be fulfilled to ensure a complete application, as well as template documents.

Compliance programme

The development of guidelines can help encourage the adoption of competition compliance programmes in Tunisia. The following elements should be considered when developing compliance programme guidelines:

- Indicate the benefits of compliance programmes, including whether they are considered a mitigating or aggravating circumstance for the purpose of setting fines.
- Recognise that there is no one-size-fits-all approach to compliance programmes, and therefore each firm should implement its own programme taking into account its size, sector of activity and the risks it faces in its day-to-day operations.
- Highlight the importance of management commitment, risk assessment, transparency and documentation, training, reporting mechanisms, as well as regular evaluation and update.
- Provide businesses with template documents that can serve as a starting point for developing compliance programmes.
- Reach out to companies to explain their obligations under competition law and to promote the adoption of compliance programmes in all economic sectors.

While competition guidelines can play an important role in fostering competition policy in Tunisia, this should go hand in hand with addressing specific shortcomings in the enforcement and advocacy frameworks. In this context, this report reiterates the relevant recommendations made in the Peer Review, providing additional elements to be taken into account by the Tunisian government.

1 Introduction

Competition policy provides firms with the right conditions and incentives to perform efficiently and innovate, to the ultimate benefit of consumers, the national economy and society. A competitive economic environment helps boost economic growth and increase living standards, thereby also contributing to reduce inequality. It stimulates competitiveness by giving businesses incentives to be more productive and reduce their prices, to better respond to customers' needs and to be more innovative. Furthermore, it motivates firms to supply internationally competitive products and services and to upgrade in global value chains.

Competition authorities tackle unlawful agreements between competitors intended to raise prices as well as abusive practices by dominant firms to exclude smaller, innovative or more efficient companies from the market. At the same time, competition authorities promote a level playing field in markets by advocating for the removal of restrictions in laws and regulations, and by prohibiting or imposing remedies on restrictive mergers.

To better achieve these objectives, competition guidelines are common instruments adopted by competition authorities worldwide. Such documents aim to articulate competition authorities' enforcement policy and approach with respect to various provisions of their competition laws, including both substantive and procedural elements. As such, they provide guidance on the application of competition law to the authority' officials, market players, other government agencies, the Judiciary, the legal community, and society.

Guidelines are of fundamental importance to companies. They enable firms to assess their position and behaviour by applying the same criteria as the administrative authority. In the eyes of businesses, guidelines increase the transparency of administrative action, help to clarify the scope of certain provisions as interpreted by the authority, create legitimate expectations, e.g. concerning consistency in the application of the competition rules, and thus increase legal certainty.

The OECD has a long tradition of reviewing competition law and policy regimes in jurisdictions across the world and providing recommendations for further improvement to policymakers and competition authorities. In the 2022 OECD Peer Review of Competition Law and Policy in Tunisia (hereafter the Peer Review), the OECD reviewed and compared Tunisia's competition law and practices with international best practices and identified areas for improvement and reform. The need to develop public guidelines to enhance legal certainty and predictability of action by the Tunisian competition authorities was among the 65 recommendations made by the peers. This report builds on the previous analysis, reviewing Tunisia's draft merger guidelines and provides insights for the Tunisian authorities to consider when developing guidelines on setting fines, leniency programmes and compliance programmes.

This report aims to contribute to Tunisia's ongoing endeavours to promote competition within its economy. Other initiatives include the OECD's 2019 competition assessment of the country's wholesale and retail trade sectors, and road and maritime freight transport, the OECD's 2022 Peer Review of Tunisia's Competition Law and Policy, the OECD 2023 competition assessment of the tourism sector and the OECD 2023 competition market study of the retail banking sector.

2 General context and scope

Tunisia submitted its competition law and policy to an OECD Peer Review in 2022 taking an important step and demonstrating its dedication to implementing a modern and effective competition law and policy framework. This report builds on the recommendations made in the Peer Review, in order to support the Tunisian Competition Authorities to improve the Tunisian competition regime. To that purpose, the report provides Tunisia with suggestions and guidance on how to address specific shortcomings, in particular through the development of competition guidelines. This section provides an introduction to the report and describes its scope and context.

2.1. Project Background

This report is part of the "Fostering competition in Tunisia" project, jointly implemented by the OECD and the *Deutsche Gesellschaft für Internationale Zusammenarbeit* (GIZ). This joint undertaking was launched in November 2022 and builds on the findings of the 2022 OECD Peer Review with a view to supporting the country in its efforts to enhance its competition enforcement and advocacy framework, including its merger control regime and judicial review process.

In addition to this report, the project included other components aiming at providing Tunisian officials with training and capacity-building activities, in order to promote the role of the competition authorities in merger review and other enforcement and advocacy areas and enhance the role of the Administrative Court in the judicial review process. In particular, the OECD organised the following seminars, with OECD staff and international experts, to Tunisian officials: (i) merger guidelines (November 2022); (ii) economics of merger control (November 2022); (iii) introduction to competition enforcement to new staff (February 2023) and (iv) cartel detection and investigation (April 2023). The OECD co-organised, together with GIZ and the EU, the first edition of Tunisia's Competition Day (*Journée de la Concurrence*) in June 2023. A high-level seminar for judges of the Administrative Court was organised in February 2024, where a set of primers for judges on key principles for competition law was presented.

2.2. Context and interplay of competition entities

Tunisia was among the first countries in Africa and the Middle East to adopt a competition law. An initial bill was produced in 1985, but it was not until July 1991 that Act No. 91-64 was finally adopted. The Act has been revised several times and was finally repealed by Act No. 2015-36 of 15 September 2015 on the reorganisation of prices and competition. Tunisia has opted for a two-pronged system comprising an independent authority – the Competition Council – and a competition department (DGCEE) within the

Ministry of Trade. The Administrative Court, which rules on appeals against the decisions of the competition bodies, completes this intuitional set-up.

The Competition Council has legal personality and financial autonomy and performs two main functions since 1995: a jurisdictional function and an advisory function. The Ministry of Trade's DGCEE is responsible for the development, implementation and enforcement of competition rules.

Although the Peer Review did not make overarching recommendations on the institutional design, it highlighted the need for a reallocation of tasks in specific areas and for a better co-ordination between both competition entities in the country.

Merger control is a concrete example. The work on the merger control guidelines pilot undertaken within this project highlighted the pressing need for the revision of tasks between the DGCEE and the Competition Council to improve the efficiency of the process. In fact, the Ministry of Trade has jurisdiction over the review and control of mergers that fulfil the conditions in Article 7 of the Competition Act No. 2015-36. However, the actual assessment of the notified operation is mainly done by the Competition Council who (only) issues a non-binding opinion. The assessment aims to determine whether the merger is likely to create or strengthen a dominant position in the domestic market or a substantial part of it. The analysis is mostly legal rather than focussed on assessing the economic impact of the concentration, and the economic analysis usually limits itself to defining market shares and the effects of the merger on the structure of the market. The opinions of the Council are usually followed by the Minister, although there have been cases in which the Minister of Trade deviated from them (OECD, 2022[1]).

Both the DGCEE and the Competition Council may conduct investigations into anti-competitive practices. To avoid the duplication of investigative efforts, Tunisian law stipulates that the Ministry of Trade must inform the Competition Council of ongoing investigations, and vice versa. An investigation into an anti-competitive practice can be triggered in one of three ways: i) a complaint from a third party, ii) a leniency application or iii) self-referral (ex officio) by the investigating authority. A leniency programme has been in place since 2003. In this respect, the competition act provides that "*the Council may, after hearing the government Commissioner, exempt from penalty or reduce the penalty for anyone who provides relevant information not accessible to the administration and likely to expose anticompetitive agreements or practices in which they took part*". Here again, both entities can be involved in the process since the application may be submitted to the DGCEE or to the general rapporteur of the Competition Council.

In terms of fine setting, the Competition Council may impose fines on companies up to 10% of their turnover in a given financial year. For individuals, the penalties include a prison sentence of 16 days to one year, a fine of TND 2 000 to TND 100 000 or both. This applies in particular to persons who have played "a decisive role" (Article 45) in the infringements set out under Article 5 of Act No. 2015-36 on competition and prices. The role of the Competition Council ends with the publishing of the decision. The Minister of Trade is responsible for implementing the decisions of the Council as well as for the recovery of fines.

The DGCEE and the Competition Council share competences in terms of competition advocacy. Article 14, paragraph 4, of Act 2015-36 stipulates that the DGCEE must co-operate with the Competition Council in "*the implementation of programmes and plans to raise awareness and promote a culture of competition*". Compliance programmes are among the key tools for developing a competition culture within companies. However, there have not been any concrete steps to promote their adoption by companies in Tunisia and there is no clear indication on which organ should play a leading role in this aspect.

The Peer Review noted that the publication of guidelines by administrative authorities is not a common practice under Tunisian law and recommended developing public guidelines to enhance legal certainty and predictability of action by both competition entities. This report aims at supporting this undertaking across the four areas discussed above.

2.3. Scope of the report

This report builds on the recommendations made in the Peer Review (OECD, 2022[1]), in order to support the Tunisian Competition Authorities to improve the Tunisian competition regime. To that purpose, this report provides Tunisia with suggestions and guidance on how to address specific shortcomings as identified in the Peer Review, in particular through the development of competition guidelines.

Chapter 3 presents general information regarding what competition guidelines are, what their benefits are and how they can be developed.

Chapters 4 to 7 deal with merger control, fining methodology, leniency programme and compliance programmes. These four areas are among the key issues where the Peer Review has suggested further actions to be implemented. These chapters provide an overview on the issues affecting the framework conditions across the four areas. Additionally, they provide an overview of selected jurisdictions' guidelines, with the view of helping Tunisian authorities when developing their own guidelines.

The seven jurisdictions selected for this study include OECD and non-OECD countries. The selection was done following a set of criteria based on the existence and accessibility of competition guidelines in the four specific areas and the extensive knowledge of the OECD about their specificities. The selected jurisdictions include:

- OECD countries: Belgium, Canada, European Union (European Commission) and France;
- Non-OECD countries: Kenya, Philippines and South Africa.

Belgium, Canada and Kenya were among the reviewers leading the Tunisia peer review process. The selection of Belgium, Canada, the European Union and France was also motivated by language considerations. The availability of their guidelines in French means that their practices are easily accessible and could be further examined by the Tunisian competition authorities, if needed. Kenya and South Africa are two key African jurisdictions with effective competition guidelines in place. The Philippine competition authority was established at the same time when the Tunisian Competition Act was revised. Furthermore, it has been an active competition enforcer and has successfully adopted a set of competition guidelines recently.

Chapter 8 provides Tunisia with recommendations to be taken into account when developing competition guidelines, in line with well-established international best practices. It also reiterates some key recommendations presented in the Peer Review that are related to the four areas covered in this report.

Given that there is a limited experience in Tunisia in terms of guidelines, a draft accompanying note on "Developing merger control guidelines" was first shared with the Tunisian authorities in February 2023 to serve as a reference for the staff tasked with producing merger guidelines as a first pilot. In September and October 2023, the Tunisian competition authorities submitted to the OECD a draft document of the Tunisian Merger Guidelines, which was taken into account in this report.

A first draft of this report was presented to Tunisian authorities in January 2024. The current report reflects all comments and suggestions received.

3 Competition guidelines

Competition guidelines are common instruments adopted by competition authorities worldwide to articulate their enforcement policy and approach with respect to various provisions of their competition laws, including both substantive and procedural elements. This section discusses competition guidelines, including their definition, potential benefits and the regulatory process to create guidelines. It also stresses how competition guidelines can be developed in Tunisia.

3.1. Definition of competition guidelines

The publication of competition guidelines by competition authorities is a common practice around the world. The term "guidelines" does not necessarily refer to their legal nature, but rather to their content. Indeed, guidelines comprise documents issued by a competition authority to spell out (often in advance and) in a transparent manner the agency's enforcement practice and approach with respect to various provisions of its competition law, including both substantive and procedural aspects, typically based on past experience. Although competition guidelines are considered rules of practice (instead of rules of law), they can have legal effect in certain circumstances, despite not being binding on the courts, as further discussed in section 3.3. As such, they provide guidance criteria on the application of competition rules to the authority' officials, market players and other stakeholders (such as other government agencies, academia and the legal community).

Competition guidelines commonly seek to explain the law; indicate how a competition authority is intending to interpret the legislative provisions; refer to any relevant case law or prior decisions, which assist the competition authority with its interpretation; and provide case or hypothetical examples.

3.2. The potential benefits of guidelines

Guidelines can serve a number of purposes for competition authorities. First, the preparation, consultation and subsequent publication of guidelines assist substantially in attaining the advocacy objectives of the competition authority to raise awareness and promote a competition culture. Second, published guidelines provide greater transparency of both the proposed substantive approach to the interpretation of the competition law and policy, as well as the competition authority's procedural requirements, which helps ensure legal certainty and predictability for businesses seeking to comply with competition law.

3.2.1. Advocacy and education

Published guidelines help guide businesses and the public on the application of competition law and are therefore a useful advocacy instrument. In addition, the consultation process on draft guidelines itself also creates an opportunity for advocacy and education. Likewise, in its *Guidelines for Implementing Competition Advocacy*, the United Nations Conference on Trade and Development (UNCTAD) notes that drafting guidelines on aspects of anti-competitive conduct or the competition process provides a useful way to engage with stakeholders (Bulgarian Commission on Protection of Competition/UNCTAD, p. 9[2]).

While guidelines are important to all competition authorities, they can play an especially critical role for countries where the competition culture is still emerging and where competition agencies are often young, inexperienced and are faced with limited resources.

3.2.2. Transparency and legal certainty for the business community

Good regulatory practice requires, amongst other things, transparency. Guidelines provide a good opportunity for competition authorities to be transparent about their approach to the interpretation of substantive competition law as well as the procedural aspects of competition enforcement.

A transparent and fair competition enforcement process ensures the impartial and reasonable treatment of subjects of competition investigations. It also improves the accuracy and comprehensiveness of competition enforcement decisions, by making sure that all arguments are heard. Observing due process reinforces the legitimacy of competition enforcement and its credibility vis-à-vis interested parties as well as all citizens.

Over the years, the OECD Competition Committee has developed extensive work on transparency and procedural fairness (OECD, 2012[3]). In 2021, the OECD Council has adopted the Recommendation on Transparency and Procedural Fairness in Competition Law Enforcement (OECD, 2021[4]). The Recommendation states that competition law enforcement should be predictable and transparent, and perceived as such by affected and interested parties, as well as citizens, ensuring public confidence in law enforcement. To this end, the Recommendation calls Adherents to develop guidelines for procedural steps in competition law enforcement.

More broadly, the OECD has identified "accountability and transparency" as one of seven principles of good governance (OECD, 2012, p. 16[5]). To ensure accountability and transparency to the public, it identifies a need for a regulator to make publicly available "key operational policies and other guidance material, covering matters such as compliance, enforcement and decision review" (OECD, 2012, p. 80[5]). By disclosing these policies and guidance material, the public should have greater confidence and understanding of what is expected of them in terms of compliance. In addition to compliance-based guidance, regulators should publish procedural guidance which discloses the "rules, data and informational inputs that will be used to make decisions" (OECD, 2012, p. 83[5]).

In this context, the publication of guidelines can help create legal certainty regarding how competition law is interpreted and applied by the competition authority. Guidelines also allow market players to examine their behaviours considering the same criteria taken into account by the competition authority.

Competition authorities being transparent about priorities, approach and interpretation of the law is crucial to create trust and establish their reputation vis-à-vis the business community. For businesses, guidelines expand the transparency of administrative action and help create legitimate expectations (for instance regarding consistency in the application of the competition rules), therefore increasing legal certainty.

3.2.3. Reflect updated practices of the competition authorities

Another benefit of guidelines is that they can be relatively easily developed and updated to reflect the practices of the agency and the jurisprudence of the courts of the land. Certainly, this is an advantage over the changing of laws and decrees, processes that are often quite difficult and take time to enact.

Accordingly, guidelines can be regularly reviewed to reflect law amendments or the evolution of the enforcement activities. For instance, many of the guidelines assessed in this report (see chapters 4 to 7) were already revised since their introduction.

Nevertheless, as guidelines only reflect a given legal framework, there are several standards that must be defined by law and therefore cannot be changed by guidelines.

3.2.4. Greater clarity to competition authorities and the judiciary

The process of drafting, consultation and issuing competition guidelines is likely to provide greater clarity for the competition authority itself in relation to the meaning and application of its competition law. Indeed, developing guidelines is an opportunity for the competition authority to think holistically about one area of competition law, consolidating its practice. The guidelines are also likely to offer assistance to the judiciary (or other appellate bodies), especially those adjudicators who may be considering competition law and economics issues for the first time.

3.3. Reliance by the regulator and judiciary

Competition guidelines typically do not have legally binding nature on courts. They are rules of practice rather than rules of law. However, the value of guidelines usually goes beyond advice, providing a clear indication of how competition authorities are likely to act.

3.3.1. The position of the competition authority in relation to published guidelines

In some jurisdictions, reference is made to the fact that guidelines as such are not legally binding in a sense that courts are not bound to them.[1] However, they may be binding on the issuing authority[2] in a sense that they are capable of producing legal effects[3] and the issuing authority cannot (lightly) disregard its own guidelines.

Competition guidelines provide guidance criteria and help create a uniform approach in the application of competition law by the authority. Competition authorities usually commit to follow their guidelines unless there are specific circumstances that justify an exemption from them.

In the European Union, for example, general principles of law (such as legitimate expectations and proportionality) apply in relation to competition law. In the context of guidelines published by the European Commission (EC), the European Court of Justice (ECJ) has held that the EC may not be able to depart from its guidelines without breaching equal treatment and legitimate expectation principles (Jones, Sufrin and Dunne, 2019, pp. 34-35[6]).

However, even if legitimate expectation or similar principles do not exist in law, the guidelines will provide a discipline for the competition authority (Commissioners and staff) in how it applies the law.

3.3.2. The reliance by the judiciary and judiciary review bodies on published guidelines

While guidelines published by the competition authority are not legally binding on the courts, they may provide a useful starting point to assist the judiciary, particularly in jurisdictions where competition law is new or substantial changes have been recently introduced.

For example, as described above, in the European Union, the ECJ has confirmed that guidelines, although not binding in the legal sense, do create a legitimate expectation and therefore "the administration may not depart in an individual case without giving reasons that are compatible with the principle of equal treatment".[4]

3.4. The regulatory process to create guidelines

Before a competition authority begins the process of creating guidelines, it would be prudent to consider what it is endeavouring to achieve: a document intended to enforce the law (such as implementing rules) or one intended to interpret or explain the law? If the former, there may be administrative rules that need to be followed to ensure the administrative issuance is valid and binding. Where the competition authority intends to issue documents that interpret or explain the law, the procedural requirements may be less formal.

Based on our research, despite there being no prescribed process, competition authorities have developed a process of their own to create and publish guidelines. The processes described by all jurisdictions are similar and can be broadly illustrated as follows:

Figure 3.1. Process to create guidelines

- **Issuance of a draft document/paper:** the competition authority publishes a draft paper outlining its proposed guidelines. Internal staff is responsible for the initial draft, if possible and desirable, with input from Commissioners and/or Board Members. In some cases, where internal knowledge is not sufficient, external consultants are relied upon. For many young authorities, existing guidelines from other regimes serve as useful material to draw from.
- **Stakeholder consultation:** the competition authority holds a public consultation period during which stakeholders can provide feedback on the proposed guidelines. This may include written submissions, public hearings, and meetings with interested parties. This may include the organisation of an event to collect oral feedback on the proposed guidelines. It is generally advisable to consult widely, using a large and diverse set of stakeholders, and ensure sufficient time for feedback. This process will increase the understanding of, and buy-in for, the guidelines – and more generally the competition law regime.
- **Review of submissions:** the competition authority reviews the submissions received during the consultation period and makes any necessary revisions to the proposed guidelines, although it is not common for the competition authority to provide feedback on submissions.
- **Finalisation and publication:** once the competition authority is satisfied with the final version of the guidelines, they are published and made available to the public.
- **Review and updates:** guidelines are reviewed and updated periodically to reflect changes in the legal and economic environment, and to ensure that they are still relevant and effective in achieving their intended purposes.

3.5. Competition guidelines in Tunisia

As mentioned above, the Peer Review recommended that Tunisia should develop public guidelines to enhance legal certainty and predictability of action by competition authorities.

According to the Peer Review, the publication of guidelines by administrative authorities is not a common practice under Tunisian law, and statutes or regulations are usually used to set out criteria or principles, for instance to indicate the stages of certain decision-making processes (OECD, 2022, p. 148[1]).

Although currently there are no national competition guidelines, the adoption of guidelines is not unprecedented in Tunisia. Indeed, the National Telecommunications Authority (INT) has adopted guidelines in 2012, 2015 and 2019 regarding the operation of public telecommunications networks (OECD, 2022, pp. 149-150[1]). Additionally, COMESA has published merger guidelines on supranational level (COMESA, 2014[7]).

Moreover, guidelines do exist even in jurisdictions where independent authorities do not have the power to issue such documents. In those cases, they are adopted by ministerial order (OECD, 2022, p. 149[1]).

It should also be noted that Article 14, paragraph 4, of Act 2015-36 establishes that the relevant departments of the Ministry of Trade must co-operate with the Competition Council in the "implementation of programmes and plans to raise awareness and promote a culture of competition", which could include the publication of guidelines.

To help Tunisian authorities to implement this recommendation, Chapters 4 to 7 provide more details on competition guidelines on merger control, fining methodology, leniency programme and compliance programme. In particular, these sections present a comparative analysis of guidelines in these areas in selected jurisdictions, including some features that Tunisian authorities may take into account when developing their own guidelines.

4 Merger control

Merger review helps avoid anti-competitive economic concentrations and is a key component of competition regimes. Merger guidelines play a crucial role in ensuring an effective merger control regime and can be particularly useful in younger competition regimes, where the competition culture is still emerging. The Tunisian competition law framework regarding merger review has a series of limitations, including a very high turnover-based notification threshold and the absence of two-phase and simplified merger control regime, as well as the lack of merger notification forms. Tunisia is currently seeking to implement merger guidelines and a draft was submitted to the OECD. This section presents an overview of merger guidelines in selected jurisdictions and reviews Tunisia's draft guidelines on merger control.

4.1. Overview of merger control in Tunisia

According to Article 7 of Act No. 2015-36 of 15 September 2015, a prior authorisation from the Minister of Trade is required for any proposed merger likely to create or strengthen a dominant position in the domestic market or a substantial part of thereof. The Tunisian merger control regime provides two alternative overall notification thresholds (i.e., referring to the merging firms together): a turnover-based test (turnovers exceeding TND 100 million in the domestic market) and a market share test (combined market share of 30% in the domestic market).

As pointed out by the Peer Review, the number of merger notifications in Tunisia is substantially lower than in other jurisdictions, for instance over 22 times lower than the MEA average in 2022 (OECD, 2024[8]). This is partially explained by the turnover-based threshold, which is too high vis-à-vis Tunisia's current economic situation (OECD, 2022, pp. 105-106[1]).

The turnover-based threshold in force in Tunisia represented 0.0771% of the GDP in 2021. The table below summarises the selected jurisdictions examined in this report, including their GDP's, their turnover notification thresholds, as well as the turnover notification thresholds as a percentage of GDP. These figures present how they can compare to the size of their economies, considered by using the GDP of such jurisdictions. They confirm that turnover-based threshold in Tunisia is indeed too high.

Table 4.1. Turnover notification thresholds in selected jurisdictions and their % of GDP in 2021

Jurisdiction	GDP 2021 (current USD in millions)	Threshold Level (USD)	% of GDP
Tunisia	46 687	36 010 000	0.0771
		Selected OECD members	
Belgium*	594 104	118 300 000	0.0199
		47 320 000	0.0079
Canada**	1 988 336	319 120 000	0.0160
		74 195 400	0.0037
European Union***	17 177 419	5 915 000 000	0.0344
		295 750 000	0.0017
France****	2 957 880	177 450 000	0.0059
		59 150 000	0.0019
		Selected non-OECD members	
Kenya*****	110 347	9 100 000	0.0082
		910 000	0.0008
Philippines******	394 086	101 500 000	0.0257
		40 600 000	0.0103
South Africa*******	419 015	40 620 000	0.0097
		6 770 000	0.0016

Note: Some of the threshold levels above consider both individual and combined assets for all the parties involved in the transaction while others only require one of the parties to meet the threshold.
* Belgium has one threshold for the local size of all the merging parties and one for each of at least two of the parties concerned (in addition, the transaction must not fall within the jurisdiction of the European Commission).
** Canada has one threshold for the local size of all the merging parties and one for the size of the transaction.
*** The EU has one threshold for the worldwide size of all the merging parties and one for EU size for each of at least two of the parties concerned. There is also a second alternative involving lower thresholds.
**** France has one threshold for the worldwide size of all the merging parties and one for the local size for each of at least two of the parties concerned (in addition, the transaction must not fall within the jurisdiction of the European Commission). There are also specific lower thresholds applicable to mergers in the retail sector and to mergers in certain French overseas territories.
***** Kenya has one threshold for the local size of all the merging parties and one for the local size of the target undertaking. There are also specific thresholds for mergers in the healthcare, carbon based mineral and oil sectors. Transactions meeting the COMESA merger notification threshold are excluded from notification if at least two-thirds of the turnover or assets (whichever in higher) is not generated or located in Kenya.
****** The Philippines has one threshold for the local size of all the merging parties and one for the size of the transaction.
******* South Africa has one threshold for the local size of all the merging parties and one for the size of the transferred/target firm. These numbers refer to so-called "intermediate mergers". There are also higher thresholds for so-called "larger mergers".
Source: World Bank, https://data.worldbank.org/indicator/NY.GDP.MKTP.CD?name_desc=false and competition authorities' website. Exchange rates (2021 average): TND 1 = USD 0.3601; CAD 1 = 0.7978; EUR 1 = USD 1.183; KES 1 = USD 0.0091; PHP 1 = USD 0.0203; ZAR 1 = USD 0.0677.

The turnover-based threshold is also too high when considering the size of companies operating in Tunisia. According to the OECD Economic Surveys: Tunisia 2018, once they are created, Tunisian firms tend to stay small, vis-à-vis the major constraints on market access, restrictive regulations, heavy taxation and problems in accessing financing (OECD, 2018, p. 66[9]). In fact, Tunisia had 828 821 firms in 2021, of which only 0.2% had more than 100 employees and less than 0.1% had more than 200 employees (Statistiques Tunisie, 2022, p. 17[10]).

Figure 4.1 displays the turnover distribution of the 100 biggest companies in Tunisia, indicating that only 88 companies have a turnover of more than TND 100 million, the current turnover notification threshold. This implies that only 88 out of more than 800 thousand companies in Tunisia would have to notify a transaction, confirming that the current turnover notification threshold is indeed set too high.

Figure 4.1. Distribution of the turnover (TND) of Tunisia's top 100 companies, 2019

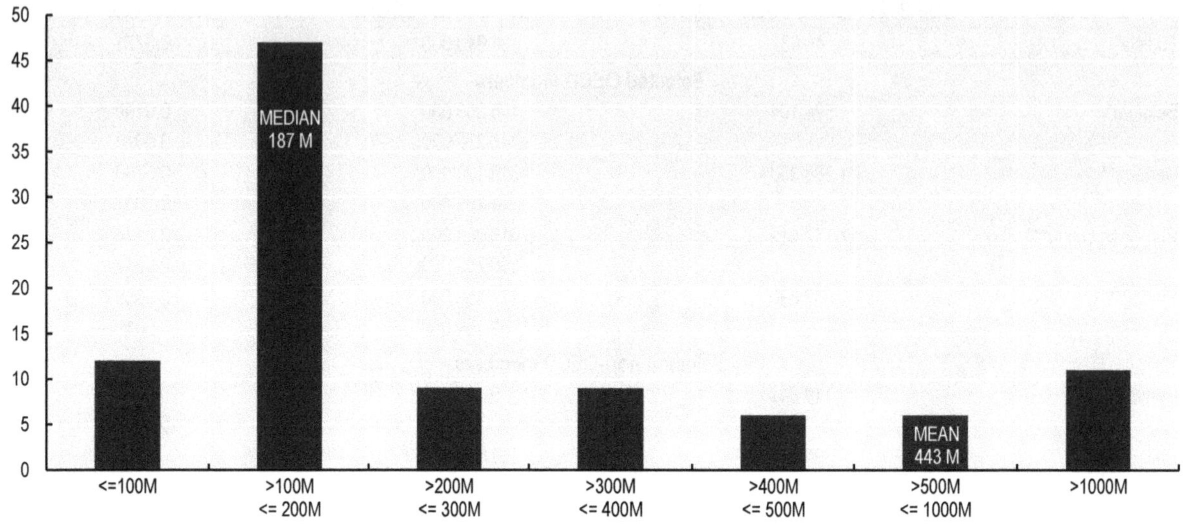

Source: OECD based on data from *L'Économiste Maghrébin* ranking of Tunisian businesses.

Although the market share-based threshold could cover transactions that are not captured by the high turnover-based threshold, determining market shares at the notification stage may be challenging and is likely to lead to legal uncertainty and high costs for companies, as highlighted in the Peer Review (OECD, 2022, p. 104[1]). Moreover, in practice the market share-based threshold has not been effective in capturing anti-competitive transactions that do not meet the turnover-based threshold in Tunisia.

In addition, while the Minister of Trade is the competent authority to approve mergers, the Competition Council shall issue a non-binding opinion, advising the Minister, who can then (i) authorise the transaction; (ii) authorise the transaction subject to remedies; or (iii) block the transaction.

The competitive assessment focuses on whether a transaction will create or strengthen a dominant position, coupled with public interest considerations (in particular, the benefits of the transaction in terms of technical or economic progress and industrial policy objectives).

From 2015 to 2021, 34 mergers were notified to the Ministry of Trade, of which 30 were cleared without conditions, three were authorised subject to remedies, and one was blocked.

The insurance, microfinance, banking and audio-visual sectors are derogated from the general merger control regime by specific legislations, which establish special regimes for such sectors. In the insurance, microfinance and banking sectors, specific regulations give another authority the competence to review and approve mergers: the Minister of Finance (insurance and microfinance sectors) and the Licensing Commission, following an opinion prepared by the Central Bank of Tunisia (banking sector). In the case of mergers in the banking sector, the Competition Council is not even consulted, while there have been no mergers in the insurance and microfinance sectors. Moreover, there is an almost absolute prohibition of consolidation in the audio-visual sector (OECD, 2022, pp. 126-131[1]).

As the Peer Review indicated, Tunisia does not have two-phase or simplified merger control regime, which contributes to the long duration of merger review.

Moreover, there are no official merger notification forms in Tunisia, which could reduce discretion of what competition authorities may request merging parties during the merger review procedures. Merger notification forms are commonly implemented by competition authorities, spelling out the required information and documents that merging parties must submit within the merger notification. While they do not prevent competition authorities from requesting additional documents at a later stage, notification forms increase predictability to merging parties and tend to reduce the length of merger reviews. This is because the basic information will always be provided at the start of the process, and merging parties can collect the required information in advance of the administrative procedure. Notification forms usually vary according to whether they refer to a simplified or complex transaction. Many jurisdictions have introduced merger notification forms, including the jurisdictions selected for comparison in this report (i.e. Belgium, Canada, European Union, France, Kenya, the Philippines, and South Africa).

According to Article 43(2) of Act No. 2015-36, if companies implement the transaction prior to notification and approval when it fulfils the conditions listed in Article 7(3) of Act No. 2015-36 (so-called gun jumping), they may be fined up to 10% of their turnover in Tunisia, regardless of whether the failure to notify a notifiable transaction was unintentional or due to negligence. While Tunisian rules related to gun jumping seem to be in line with international best practices, the absence of enforcement deviates from the international practices. Indeed, while gun-jumping enforcement has been increased worldwide, Tunisian competition authorities have never sanctioned companies for such an infringement, even though non-notified transactions that fulfilled notification thresholds were identified (OECD, 2022, p. 106[1]).

Finally, notification of a merger is not subject to a notification fee in Tunisia, which could be one alternative that could increase the competition authorities' budget (which in turn could be used to improve human resources) (OECD, 2022, p. 108[1]).

4.2. Merger control guidelines

Merger guidelines play a crucial role in ensuring an effective merger control regime and can be particularly useful in younger competition regimes, where the competition culture is still emerging. Merger guidelines outline the processes and considerations that competition authorities should take into account when reviewing proposed mergers and acquisitions. They also provide guidance on how to evaluate the potential effects of a merger on competition, including on market structure, pricing, and innovation.

Merger guidelines help competition authorities by providing a framework for evaluating the potential competitive effects of a proposed merger or acquisition. The content of merger guidelines can vary across competition authorities, often depending on the experience of the competition authority and the business community with merger control. They typically explain the most relevant concepts, elaborate on the general procedural steps and explore the criteria used to evaluate proposed mergers. Merger guidelines usually specify the types of information or analysis that authorities will typically consider when assessing a merger, including market definition, market concentration, barriers to entry, and the potential for co-ordinated or unilateral effects. This helps authorities to identify and investigate potentially problematic mergers, and to make informed decisions about whether to approve or challenge a proposed transaction. Additionally, as described in chapter 3, merger guidelines can also help provide transparency and predictability for merging or acquiring businesses, as they can better understand the types of factors that will be considered in a merger review. This is in line with the OECD Recommendation on Merger Review, which states that jurisdictions should ensure that the rules, policies and procedures involved in the merger review process are transparent and publicly available (OECD, 2005[11]).

This section considers the elements commonly covered in merger guidelines by comparing guidelines published in the selected jurisdictions.[5] It also considers the draft Tunisian Merger Guidelines submitted by the Tunisian competition authorities to the OECD in September and October 2023.

In 2004, the International Competition Network (ICN) published a report following a review of the merger guidelines in operation at that time (ICN, 2004[12]), later complemented in 2006 (ICN, 2006[13]). The key elements of the guidelines identified in those reports have been used as an inspiration for the comparative table of merger guidelines in selected jurisdictions (Table A A.2). A list of the merger guidelines in the selected jurisdictions is set out in Table A A.1.

4.2.1. Overview of guidelines reviewed

The project team has assessed the merger guidelines the selected jurisdictions, listed in Table A A.1 and summarised in Table 4.2.

Table 4.2. Overview of guidelines reviewed

Jurisdiction	Number of guidelines	Substantive	Procedural	Combined	Date of first guideline	Date of commencement of merger regime
OECD countries						
Belgium*	-	-	-	-	-	1991
Canada	5	1	3	1	1991	1910
European Union	6	4	2	-	2003	1989
France	1	-	-	1	2004	1977
Non-OECD countries						
Kenya	2	1	-	1	2021	2010
Philippines	4	1	2	1	2016	2015
South Africa**	3	1	2	-	2016	1979

Note: * In Belgium, the European Commission's Best Practices Guidelines on merger control are applied by analogy until the Belgium Competition Authority adopts specific guidelines (Belgian Competition Authority, 2023[14]).
** South Africa's substantive guidelines refer only to the evaluation of public interest grounds in merger review.

4.2.2. Horizontal versus non-horizontal mergers

There was a mixed approach to the treatment of horizontal and non-horizontal mergers in the guidelines. Most jurisdictions (Canada, France and Kenya) combine both horizontal and non-horizontal issues in their guidelines, while the European Union has issued separate guidelines. The Philippine guidelines focus on horizontal mergers. However, it is stated that the "underlying principles can also be applied to non-horizontal mergers" and that the PCC intends to release guidance on non-horizontal mergers in the future (Philippine Competition Commission, 2018, p. 6[15]). The draft Tunisian Merger Guidelines expressly indicates that they apply to horizontal and non-horizontal mergers, although it is not explained how the competition assessment varies in each type of transaction.

Table 4.3. Horizontal and non-horizontal mergers

Jurisdiction	Horizontal	Non-Horizontal	Combined
OECD countries			
Canada			✓
European Union	✓	✓	
France			✓
Non-OECD countries			
Kenya			✓
Philippines	✓		

4.2.3. Common features of guidelines reviewed

More specifically, the following elements have been included in the guidelines of the selected jurisdictions, as summarised in Table 4.4.

Table 4.4. Summary of common features in merger guidelines in selected jurisdictions

Jurisdiction	Introductory statements	Definition of merger	Notification thresholds	Market definition	Merger test and factors	Competition effects		Remedies	Use of examples
						Unilateral	Co-ordinated		
OECD countries									
Canada	✓	✓	✓*	✓	✓	✓	✓	✓*	✓
European Union	✓	✓	✓*	✓*	✓	✓	✓	✓*	✓
France	✓	✓	✓	✓	✓	✓	✓	✓	✓
Non-OECD countries									
Kenya	✓	✓	✓	✓*	✓	✓	✓	✓	✓
Philippines	✓	✓	✓*	✓	✓	✓	✓	✓	✓

Note: * Refer to separate guidelines.

Introductory statements

Most guidelines include introductory words that set the scene for the application of merger law in the particular jurisdiction. Such introductory statements include the objective of the guidelines, as well as the way in which they have been developed.

For example, the Canadian Merger Enforcement Guidelines state that they aim at providing "general direction on its [the Competition Bureau] analytical approach to merger review" (Competition Bureau, 2011, p. 1[16]). The Merger Control Guidelines of the *Autorité de la concurrence* affirm that they intend to provide "guidance on the merger control procedures and practice" of the authority (Autorité de la concurrence, 2020, p. 1[17]). The Kenyan Merger Guidelines highlights that they intend to "improve the business regulatory framework and enhance business environment" (Competition Authority of Kenya, n.d., p. 2[18])

In younger regimes, the introductory part usually also includes an emphasis on the rationale for merger review. For instance, the Philippines explains the rationale for merger review at the beginning of its substantive guidelines (Philippine Competition Commission, 2018, p. 2[15]).

The draft Tunisian Merger Guidelines include an introduction outlining their objectives, which include clarify merger control rules, providing greater transparency and fairness to businesses, as well as improve merger control process. The draft guidelines also highlight the importance of merger control in general.

Definition of merger

Most guidelines explain what is considered a merger for the purpose of merger control, spelling out the more general definitions provided for in the legislation, for instance the difference between a merger, acquisition and consolidation and the types of share acquisitions, asset sales and participating interests. The draft Tunisian Merger Guidelines also include a section explaining the concept of mergers, in line with Act No. 2015-36 of 15 September 2015.

Notification thresholds

Most guidelines explain the notification thresholds that are applicable in the relevant jurisdiction. The way in which such thresholds are treated in guidelines can differ considerably, mostly due to the different nature of the respective merger systems (compulsory or voluntary merger regime).

The draft Tunisian Merger Guidelines refer to the two existing notification thresholds, as provided for by Act No. 2015-36 of 15 September 2015.

Market definition

Given the central role of market definition in most merger cases, many guidelines elaborate on the role of market definition, the way in which markets are defined and how they may change the outcome of a merger review. While many merger guidelines discuss market definition in detail (e.g., Canada and France), some refer to separate guidelines that deal with market definition (e.g., the EU and Kenya). All define markets by reference to product and geographic dimensions and refer to the hypothetical monopolist test to define markets.

The draft Tunisian Merger Guidelines include a short description of market definition, without detailing how the competition authorities assess this in practice. Providing further elements in this regard could be useful for increasing legal certainty and ensure that market players understand how competition law in interpreted and applied. This is particularly relevant considering that one of the notification thresholds is based on a market share test, which can be challenging for merging parties and lead to considerable uncertainty about whether the transaction is notifiable, as indicated in the Peer Review (OECD, 2022, p. 104[1]).

Applicable substantive merger test and relevant factors

Most merger guidelines contain an explanation of the relevant merger test and the factors that will be considered in determining the competitive effects of a merger. For instance, relevant factors include the market structure, the market position of market players, the availability of substitutes and their ability to access the market, switching costs, and other barriers to entry. Most jurisdictions use a "with and without" (or "counterfactual") test to determine whether the relevant merger test is met. This means that an analysis is conducted of a situation with and without the merger.

As highlighted in the Peer Review, currently the competitive assessment of mergers in Tunisia is based mostly on a legal analysis rather than on an economic assessment of the effects of the merger, being essentially limited to defining market shares and the effects of the merger on the structure of the market. In this regard, the Peer Review recommended the introduction of a substantial lessening of competition (SLC) test for merger analysis, in addition to a test based on creating or increasing a dominant position (OECD, 2022[1]). The draft Tunisian Merger Guidelines mention that the assessment carried out by the Competition Council considers the impact of the transaction on competition, while the DGCEE rests on whether the merger is likely to create or strengthen a dominant position in the relevant market or a substantial part of it.

Competition effects

Most jurisdictions identify the key competition concerns with mergers as unilateral (called "non-coordinated" in some jurisdictions) or co-ordinated effects. Unilateral effects arise where the merged entity can exercise unilateral market power with adverse effects on competition and co-ordinated effects arise where, as a result of the merger, co-ordination among firms is easier, more likely, more stable or more effective.

The draft Tunisian Merger Guidelines mention that the Competition Council considers competition effects, including unilateral and co-ordinated effects. However, as mentioned above, the competition assessment carried out by the DGCEE is based on structural considerations and therefore do not include competition effects.

Remedies

All guidelines analysed in this report deal with merger remedies, although the level of details can vary significantly. Some competition authorities have published separate guidelines to elaborate on merger remedies. For example, this is the case in Canada (Competition Bureau, 2006[19]) and the European Union (European Commission, 2008[20]). In other regimes (such as France and Kenya), the merger guidelines explain the concepts of structural and behavioural remedies, as well as how remedies can be procedurally implemented. In the Philippines, the possible structural and behavioural remedies are outlined relatively briefly in the guidelines.

The draft Tunisian Merger Guidelines mention that mergers can be authorised subject to conditions, which can be structural or behavioural. They also indicate the conditions remedies must fulfil (e.g. effective, clear, quickly implementable, capable of being monitored and proportionate to addressing the competitive harm).

It is also stated that structural remedies are preferable to behavioural remedies. However, these elements are only briefly discussed and could be further described.

Use of examples

Including case and/or hypothetical examples in merger guidelines can be useful. Such examples can illustrate certain concepts or more concrete on how a merger would be assessed.

For instance, the Merger Control Guidelines of the *Autorité de la concurrence* present several examples, including administrative and judicial caselaw, to illustrate how the topics have been addressed in practice in previous cases (Autorité de la concurrence, 2020[17]).

The draft Tunisian Merger Guidelines only include examples related to previous cases where the Competition Council has issued an opinion either to block the transaction or approve it subject to remedies. However, the document does not indicate the final decision of the DGCEE, nor provide details on the analysis carried out by the Competition Council. Additional and more detailed examples, either hypothetical or practical could be particularly relevant to illustrate how the competition authorities have interpreted and applied competition law.

4.2.4. Less common but helpful features of guidelines reviewed

The review revealed less common but helpful features in the guidelines in the selected jurisdictions which are worth mentioning. A summary of these features is set out in Table 4.5.

Table 4.5. Less common but helpful features of merger guidelines

Jurisdiction	Legally non-binding nature	Terminology	Safe harbours	Joint ventures	Ancillary restraints
			OECD countries		
Canada	✓		✓		
European Union	Implied		✓	✓	✓*
France	Implied		✓	✓	✓
			Non-OECD countries		
Kenya	✓	✓		✓*	
Philippines	Implied			✓*	✓

Note: * Refer to separate guidelines.

Legally non-binding nature of guidelines

Competition authorities may wish to consider making express statements about the legally non-binding nature of guidelines on courts, although it is implied in some jurisdictions.

For example, both the EU Guidelines on horizontal and non-horizontal mergers indicate that the Commission's interpretation of the Merger Regulation "is without prejudice to the interpretation which may be given by the Court of Justice or the Court of First Instance of the European Communities" (European Commission, 2008[21]; European Commission, 2008[22]). That said, as mentioned in section 3.3.1, in some circumstances, guidelines can have legal effect and may be binding on the issuing competition authority – unless stated otherwise.

For instance, the Merger Control Guidelines of the *Autorité de la concurrence* recognise that "the Autorité commits to apply the guidelines whenever it examines a merger, provided that there are no circumstances specific to the merger or any considerations in the general interest that would justify an exemption from them" (Autorité de la concurrence, 2020, p. 1[17]).

The Kenyan Merger Guidelines stress that they "do not have the force of law and is not binding on the Tribunal or any court of law" (Competition Authority of Kenya, n.d.[18]).

The Philippines does not expressly affirm that the guidelines are non-binding but does state that the PCC will apply the guidelines "flexibly, or where appropriate, deviate therefrom" (Philippine Competition Commission, 2018, p. 1[15]).

The draft Tunisian Merger Guidelines do not mention their non-binding nature, which could be relevant considering that the issuance of guidelines is not a common administrative practice.

Terminology

Some guidelines include explanations of relevant terminology, usually in the form of a glossary. This assists the business community and can be particularly useful in jurisdictions where merger review is new or less effective. For example, in Kenya, merger guidelines present a glossary of relevant terms (Competition Authority of Kenya, n.d., p. 60[18]).

The draft Tunisian Merger Guidelines do not include a session with relevant terms. This could increase the understanding of merger control regime.

Safe harbours

Inclusion of any applicable "safe harbours" can be a particularly useful tool to assist businesses to understand when their mergers may not give rise to competition concerns. The OECD Recommendation on Merger Review recommends the adoption of procedures to ensure that merger that do not raise material competitive concerns are subject to expedited review and clearance (OECD, 2005[11]).

For example, the European Commission states that a horizontal merger where the market share of the undertakings concerned does not exceed 25% in the common market (or a substantial part of it) may be presumed to be compatible with the common market. Moreover, the Commission is unlikely to identify horizontal competition concerns in a market with a post-merger HHI below 1 000 (European Commission, 2008[21]).[6] As regards non-horizontal mergers, the European Commission indicates that it is unlikely to find concern in non-horizontal mergers where the market share post-merger of the new entity in each of the markets concerned is below 30% and the post-merger HHI is below 2 000 (European Commission, 2008[22]).[7]

The Canadian Merger Enforcement Guidelines also establish particular thresholds to distinguish mergers that are unlikely to have anti-competitive effects from those that require an in-depth analysis. For instance, mergers leading to market share of the merged firm less than 35% generally will not be challenged based on a concern related to the unilateral exercise of market power. In addition, the competition authority generally will not challenge a merger based on a concern related to a co-ordinated exercise of market power when the post-merger market share of the four largest players in the market would be less than 65% or the post-merger market share of the merged entity would be less than 10% (Competition Bureau, 2011, pp. 18-19[16]).

The Peer Review recommended that Tunisia should create a simplified procedure for notification of simpler mergers that do not raise competition concerns (OECD, 2022, p. 170[1]). The merger guidelines could thus address this issue by establishing "safe harbours" to indicate which cases would not be likely to raise competition concerns, possibly be subject to a simplified procedure. Nevertheless, this is not the case of the draft Tunisian Merger Guidelines.

Joint ventures

The approach to assessing joint ventures may be an area of great diversity among competition authorities. This diversity stems from differences in what relevant legal frameworks consider constitutes a transaction. Considering the differences in legal definitions of a transaction, including a joint venture, it may be helpful for a competition authority to state clearly its position on how to assess joint ventures under the merger regime in its guidelines. For instance, Kenya and the Philippines have developed separate guidelines on notification of joint ventures (Competition Authority of Kenya, 2021[23]; Philippine Competition Commission, 2018[24]).

As indicated in the Peer Review, Tunisian Competition Act does not explicitly define whether the creation of a joint venture is considered a merger, although the competition authorities indicate that this is the case if they perform on a lasting basis an autonomous economic entity (OECD, 2022, pp. 102-103, 170[1]). The draft Tunisian Merger Guidelines clarify that the creation of a joint venture performing on a lasting basis all the functions of an autonomous economic entity is considered a merger, which might provide business with greater certainty whether their transactions are subject to a notification requirement.

Ancillary restraints

Some of the merger guidelines reviewed also focus on ancillary restraints (i.e., the restrictions directly related and necessary to the implementation of the transaction).

The European Commission has separate guidelines on ancillary restraints (European Commission, 2005[25]), while the *Autorité de la concurrence* has included the topic in the same document (Autorité de la concurrence, 2020, pp. 224-226[17]). In the Philippines, ancillary restraints are briefly mentioned in the merger guidelines and appear to be covered by the merger review (Philippine Competition Commission, 2018, p. 7[15]).

The draft Tunisian Merger Guidelines have no reference to ancillary restraints.

Key takeaways – Merger control

- Merger review helps avoid anti-competitive economic concentrations and is a key component of competition regimes. Merger guidelines play a crucial role in ensuring an effective merger control regime and can be particularly useful in younger competition regimes, where the competition culture is still emerging.
- The Tunisian competition law framework regarding merger review has a series of limitations, including a very high turnover-based notification threshold and the absence of two-phase and simplified merger control regime, as well as the lack of merger notification forms.
- While Tunisia is currently seeking to implement merger guidelines, the draft submitted to the OECD has some shortcomings, in particular:
  - There is no substantial guidance as regards market definition and the setting of remedies.
  - While it applies to horizontal and non-horizontal mergers, there are not elements on how the competition assessment varies in each type of transaction.
  - The competition assessment carried out by the Competition Council considers the impact of the transaction on competition, while the DGCEE focuses on whether the merger is likely to create or strengthen a dominant position in the relevant market or a substantial part of it.
  - There are only few and brief examples and reference to previous cases.
  - It does not state the legally non-binding nature of the guidelines on courts.
  - There are no "safe harbours" to indicate which cases are unlikely to raise competition concerns.

5 Fining methodology

Fines play key a role in deterrence by making unlawful conduct less profitable. Adopting public rules or guidelines about the setting of pecuniary penalties may enhance general deterrence by allowing companies to understand how heavy the sanctions to which they may be subject are. The Tunisian competition law framework regarding fines is overall in line with international standards. However, there is no established fining methodology. This section presents an overview of fining methodology guidelines in selected jurisdictions, aiming to help Tunisian authorities to implement their own guidelines.

5.1. Overview of competition law sanctions in Tunisia

According to Article 43 of Act 2015-36, fines imposed by the Competition Council on anti-competitive infringements must be up to 10% of the turnover taken in Tunisia by the operator concerned in the last financial year. Act 2015-36 has increased the maximum fining cap, which previously was fixed at 5%.

However, as pointed out be by Peer Review, in many infringement decisions no pecuniary sanctions are applied. While this used to be more common in the past, there are still some cases where no fines have been imposed (OECD, 2022, pp. 91-92[1]). This significantly reduces deterrence effects, also contributing for low incentives for competition law infringers to use leniency applications, as mentioned in chapter 6.

Evidence from OECD's CompStats database shows that the total amount of pecuniary sanctions imposed by the Competition Council over the 2015-2022 period was largely below the regional average of fines imposed in the Middle East and Africa (MEA).

Figure 5.1. Amount of fines (EUR) imposed in Tunisia compared to MEA regional average

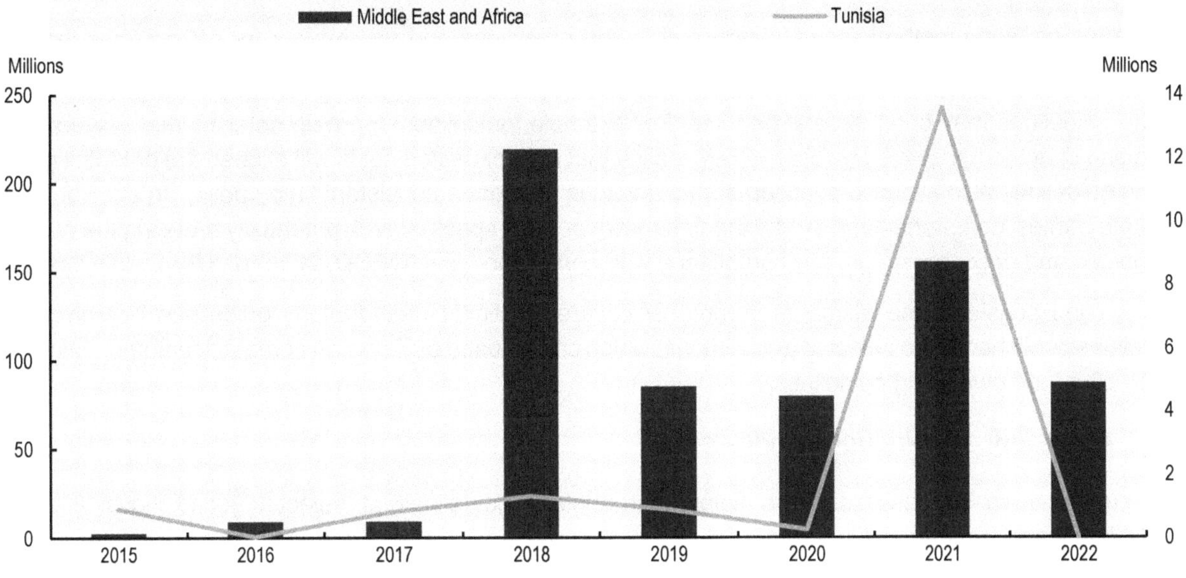

Source: OECD COMPSTATS database.

Competition law offenders are often subject to fines which impose a cost on those companies or individuals undertaking illegal anticompetitive conduct. Fines play a role in deterrence by making unlawful conduct less profitable. Breaking competition laws is profitable if it goes undetected. From the perspective of a pure profit-maximising company, it will not violate the law if the expected monetary sanctions (discounted by the probability of that fine actually being imposed) are greater than the expected illegal gain.

In Tunisia, there is no established clear fining methodology. For instance, the Peer Review has recommended that Tunisia should consider the duration of the infringement when setting fines. An established methodology on setting fines could help Tunisian competition authorities ensure a consistent fining policy. This would reduce discretion of administrative authorities when setting fines, which could be useful in judicial review, as courts could rely on an objective procedure previously established.

Decisions issued by the Competition Council can be appealed before the Administrative Court. Appeals have a suspensive effect on the decisions of the Competition Council, encouraging defendants to appeal. Moreover, cases before the Administrative Court last between five to ten years on average, although Article 28 of Act 2015-36 indicated that they should take no longer than one year. The same provision also states that the Competition Council can, where appropriate, order the provisional enforcement of its decisions, but this is not a common practice (OECD, 2022, pp. 132-133[1]). Even when fines are imposed by the Competition Council, they are still not deterrent, since it can take years before the firms finally pay them.

It is also worth mentioning that the Council does not have the mandate to oversee the implementation of its own decisions as it lacks representation powers before other public bodies, including the Administrative Court. In fact, the Minister of Trade is responsible for implementing the decisions of the Competition Council as well as for the recovery of fines. As such, the Council does not keep track of its decisions outcomes or the recovery of fines.

Although the improvement of the general fining framework depends on how the Tunisian authorities will deal with the above-mentioned shortcomings, adopting public rules or guidelines about the setting of pecuniary penalties – as is common in many jurisdictions – should help in many ways. It may enhance general deterrence by allowing companies to understand how heavy the sanctions to which they may be subject are. It helps ensure that there is a principled approach to ensure deterrence. It adds transparency to the competition authorities' approach and the logic underpinning it. Ultimately, public guidance on the setting of pecuniary penalties would add to legal certainty.

5.2. Fining methodology guidelines

Guidelines on fining methodology typically outline the objectives and procedures for setting fines that are imposed on market players who violate competition law, in particular as regards anti-competitive behaviour.

These guidelines may bring several benefits. For example, guidelines can help deter market players from engaging in anti-competitive practices if they realise that their expected costs will exceed the potential gains. Fining guidelines also allow competition authorities to implement a consistent fining policy. In addition, they facilitate parties' comprehension of why the fines were set at a specific level, potentially reducing the number of appeals and encouraging greater compliance with competition law (OECD, 2016, p. 37[26]).

This section considers the elements commonly covered in fining methodology guidelines by comparing guidelines published in the selected jurisdictions, which can be used by Tunisian competition authorities when developing their own fining guidelines.

5.2.1. Overview of guidelines reviewed

The project team has assessed the fining methodology guidelines of selected jurisdictions, listed in Table A A.4 and summarised in Table 5.1.

Table 5.1. Overview of guidelines reviewed

Jurisdiction	Guidelines	Date of guidelines
	OECD countries	
Belgium	-*	-
Canada	-	-
European Union	✓	2006
France	✓	2021
	Non-OECD countries	
Kenya	✓**	2020
Philippines	-	-
South Africa	✓	2015

Note: * Although Belgium has developed fining guidelines, they refer to the European Commission Guidelines, only presenting specific adaptations to the Belgian context. For this reason, they were not considered in the review carried out in this report.
** The Kenyan Guidelines also refer to sanctions for mergers implemented without prior authorisation by the competition authority and for the revocation of approval of proposed mergers. These sanctions will not be considered in this report.

5.2.2. Common features of guidelines reviewed

The following elements have been included in the guidelines of the selected jurisdictions, as summarised in Table 5.2.

Table 5.2. Summary of common features in fining methodology guidelines in selected jurisdictions

Jurisdiction	Objectives of the guidelines	Objectives of fines	Determination of basic fine	Duration of the infringement	Aggravating and mitigating circumstances	Statutory limits on fines	Inability to pay	Leniency and settlement
				OECD countries				
European Union	✓	✓	✓	✓	✓	✓	✓	✓
France	✓	✓	✓	✓	✓	✓	✓	✓
				Non-OECD countries				
Kenya	✓	✓	✓	✓	✓	✓	✓	✓
South Africa	✓	✓	✓	✓	✓	✓	✓	✓

Objectives of the guidelines

All guidelines expressly indicate their objectives. While all guidelines refer to increase of transparency, the documents also mention other goals. For example, the European Commission Guidelines seeks to "ensure transparency and impartiality of its decisions" (European Commission, 2006[27]). Likewise, the South African Guidelines state that its primary objective is "to provide some measure of transparency and objectivity in how the Commission will determine administrative penalties" (Competition Commission of South Africa, 2015, p. 6[28]). In addition to increase transparency, the French Guidelines aims to allow interested parties to better understand how pecuniary sanctions are set, enable economic players to anticipate the financial risks associated with committing offences and help judicial authorities carry out their monitoring mission more easily (Autorité de la concurrence, 2021, p. 5[29]). The Kenyan Guidelines seek to "enhance transparency, consistency and predictability in computation of the financial penalties and achieve proportionality on the remedies imposed against the degree of the contravention" (Competition Authority of Kenya, 2020, p. 3[30]).

Objectives of fines

All guidelines also specify the objectives of the fining policy. All guidelines mention deterrence of anti-competitive conduct. In particular, the guidelines from the European Commission, France and South Africa specify that deterrence involves both deterring the undertakings concerned from engaging in the same anti-competitive behaviour in the future (specific deterrence) and dissuading other undertakings from engaging in or continuing anti-competitive conduct (general deterrence).

Furthermore, the French Guidelines indicate that sanctions also seek to punish the infringers. They also expressly mention that sanctions do not seek compensation (Autorité de la concurrence, 2021, p. 4[29]).

Determination of basic amount of the fine

According to all guidelines, the first step of the fines-setting process is the determination of the basic amount, which is set by taking a proportion of the turnover or volume of affected commerce of the undertaking concerned. The gravity of the competition infringement plays a significant role in determining the basic amount of the fine imposed on competition infringers. The gravity of the infringement refers to the severity or seriousness of the anti-competitive behaviour committed by the infringing party(ies). An assessment of such gravity considers different factors, including the nature and extent of the infringement, the harm caused to competition, the duration of the infringement, and the market impact.

On the one hand, the European Commission and French guidelines refer to the value of the sales of goods or services to which the infringement relates in the relevant geographic area within the EEA or in France, respectively. This is considered to be an appropriate proxy to reflect the economic relevance of the infringement and the relative weight of each market player in the infringement (European Commission, 2006[27]; Autorité de la concurrence, 2021, p. 7[29]).

On the other hand, the Kenyan Guidelines consider the affected turnover of an undertaking in the year before the competition authority reaches a decision, which gives indication of the amount of commerce affected (Competition Authority of Kenya, 2020, p. 4[30]). Likewise, the South African Guidelines also use the concept of affected turnover, referring to the "firm's turnover derived from the sales of products and services that can be said to have been affected by the contravention" (Competition Commission of South Africa, 2015, p. 8[28]).

The guidelines also describe how the value of sales or the affected turnover is calculated, including the geographic and temporal dimensions. The guidelines also explain how this amount should be determined in cases involving associations of undertakings.

For instance, in both the European Union and France, where the infringement by an association of undertakings relates to the activities of its members, the value of sales will generally refer to the sum of the value of sales by its members (European Commission, 2006[27]; Autorité de la concurrence, 2021, p. 8[29]). In Kenya, the gross annual turnover of an association of undertakings is derived from the individual members' turnover of the products or services that are the subject of a contravention (Competition Authority of Kenya, 2020, p. 4[30]). In South Africa, in case of infringement by an association of firms and the association is responsible for aiding, organising and/or executing the infringement, it shall be liable for payment of the fine, separately from the members of the association. Under these circumstances, the total revenue/members' contributions to fees will be considered the affected turnover (Competition Commission of South Africa, 2015, p. 9[28]).

All guidelines recognise that for some infringements the value of sales or the affected turnover may not reflect the weight of each participant in the infringement, and alternative criteria is introduced to determine the basic amount of the fine.

For instance, the European Commission and French guidelines indicate that when the scope of the infringement extends beyond the EEA or France, respectively (for example, international cartels with market-sharing arrangements), the competition authority may assess the total value of the sales of goods or services to which the infringement relates in the relevant geographic area (wider than the EEA), determine the share of the sales of each participant on the market and apply this share to the aggregate sales within the EEA of the undertakings concerned (European Commission, 2006[27]; Autorité de la concurrence, 2021, p. 8[29]).

Likewise, the South African Guidelines state that where the affected turnover of a firm is zero for a particular market (e.g. in the case of market allocation precluding entry into a certain product of geographical areas), the Competition Commission may take into account the company's annual turnover in the market that was protected as a result of the practice, i.e. the market that was allocated to the firm as a result of the anti-competitive behaviour (Competition Commission of South Africa, 2015, p. 9[28]).

The French Guidelines also include other circumstances where alternative criteria can be used for determining the basic amount of the fine. For example, if the infringement consists of an agreement on commissions by which firms are remunerated for the sale of certain goods or services, the *Autorité de la concurrence* may consider these commissions as a reference. Moreover, in case of two-sided or multi-sided markets, the value of sales made by the undertaking concerned on the upstream, downstream or related markets can be considered by the competition authority, where they are directly or indirectly related to the infringement (Autorité de la concurrence, 2021, p. 8[29]).

Some guidelines also present specific rules for bid rigging cases. For example, the French Guidelines recognise that the general methodology must be adapted in cases of bid rigging, as the value of sales does not properly reflect the economic relevance of the practices and the relative weight of each participant, especially when their involvement consists of cover bidding or bid suppression. Accordingly, the basic amount should result from the application of a coefficient determined based on the gravity of the facts, the total turnover achieved in France by the undertakings or the association of undertakings, typically during the complete business year in which the offence occurred or the last complete business year if there are more than one. This coefficient will also consider that such practices are among the most serious competition violations (Autorité de la concurrence, 2021, p. 15[29]).

The Kenyan Guidelines state that in bid rigging cases the competition authority should take into account the value of the tender contract to be the affected turnover used to set the fines (Competition Authority of Kenya, 2020, p. 10[30]).

The South African Guidelines provide that, for bid rigging violations, the affected turnover of both the winning bidder and the other participants of the infringement will be considered the greater of (i) the value of the bid submitted by the winning bidder, (ii) the value of the contract concluded or to be concluded or (iii) the amount ultimately paid to the successful bidder pursuant to the tender. Additionally, for bid rigging cases the competition authority will consider the number of years for which the contract lasts as the duration of the infringement multiplier (Competition Commission of South Africa, 2015, pp. 9-10, 12[28]).

As for the percentage to be applied to the value of sales or the affected turnover, it varies according to the jurisdiction but takes into account the gravity of the infringement. For example, the guidelines from the European Commission, France and South Africa indicate that the proportion of the value of sales should be up to 30%. The guidelines provide some elements to be considered when determining which percentage should be applied at a specific case. While these factors vary across the guidelines, some common elements include the nature, gravity and extent of the infringement. Other elements indicated in some guidelines are the combined market share of all the undertakings concerned, barriers to entry in the market and the nature of the activities, sectors or markets at stake. These guidelines also mention that the percentage for hard-core cartels should generally be set at the higher end of the scale.

In Kenya, however, the percentages are pre-established at 10%. The duration of the infringement is then considered when adjusting the basic fine considering aggravating circumstances (Competition Authority of Kenya, 2020, pp. 4-7[30]).

The European Commission and French guidelines also provide that a sum of between 15% and 25% of the value of sales should be added to the basic amount in the case of hard-core cartels, to further deter companies from entering into such practices. The specific percentage should be determined taking into account the elements referred above. This additional amount can also be applied in the case of other infringements.

Duration of the infringement

The guidelines of the European Commission, France and South Africa establish that the duration of the infringement will be taken into account by multiplying the basic amount by the number of years of the participation in the anti-competitive practice. These guidelines also explain how the duration of the infringement is considered when it involves period of less than one year. On the one hand, the European Commission Guidelines state that periods up to six months are counted as half a year and periods between six months and one year will be counted as a full year. On the other hand, the French and South African guidelines provide that for infringements lasting less than one year the basic amount should be multiplied by the proportion of the year over which the practice lasted.

According to the Kenyan Guidelines, the duration of the conduct is considered only as an aggravating circumstance.

Aggravating and mitigating circumstances

According to all guidelines, the basic fine (including, when applicable, after the duration of the infringement is considered) is then adjusted by increasing or decreasing it in light of aggravating and mitigating circumstances. All guidelines present a non-exhaustive list of such circumstances.

The most common mitigating circumstances include: (i) immediate termination of the infringement following the knowledge of the competition authority's investigation (although this factor usually does not apply to secret practices, such as cartels); (ii) minor role in the anti-competitive behaviour (i.e. whether the firm was a passive participant); (iii) co-operation with the competition authority (e.g. by providing evidence concerning infringements); (iv) the infringement was authorised or motivated by public authorities or by legislation; (v) pressure exercised by other companies (e.g. whether the firm was coerced by other firms who were party to the infringement); and (vi) compensation for injured parties.[8]

As for aggravating circumstances, the following factors are referred to in most guidelines: (i) recidivism (although debate exists regarding whether it relates to the same or similar infringements and the same legal entity, as well as the limitation period of the range of prior infringements); (ii) refusal to co-operate with the competition authority (e.g. obstruction of investigations and non-compliance with procedural obligations, such as failure to reply, late replies and incomplete or misleading provision of information); (iii) role of leader in, or instigator of, the infringement; and (iv) coercion or retaliatory measures to ensure continuation of the infringement.[9]

The guidelines from the European Commission, France and South Africa do not indicate detailed elements on how much the basic amount should be reduced or increased in light of aggravating and mitigating circumstances. On the other hand, the Kenyan Guidelines provide a score system with a different percentage to increase or reduce the basic amount.

The European Commission and French guidelines also provide that in case of recidivism the basic amount should be increased up to 100% and between 15% and 50%, respectively. While the European Commission only mention "the same or a similar infringement" (European Commission, 2006[27]), France explains in more details the elements that should be considered when assessing recidivism. This includes (i) the existence of a decision from the European Commission or a competition authority from any EU Member State sanctioning practices of the same nature; (ii) the second practice is identical or similar, in its object of effects, to the second infringement; (iii) the previous sanctioning decision should be final on the date on which the competition authority sanctions the second practice; and (iv) the second infringement has started within 15 years from the date on which the first decision was issued (Autorité de la concurrence, 2021, p. 12[29]).

Statutory limits on fines

All guidelines mention and explain a maximum fining cap, established by legislation. When the fine is set beyond this amount, the competition authority must fix it at the maximum cap. All guidelines refer to a similar fining cap of 10% of the firm's annual turnover, albeit with different features.

For instance, the European Commission Guidelines indicate that the legal maximum is set at 10% of the total turnover in the preceding business year of the undertaking or association of undertakings participating in the infringement. Where infringements of an association relate to the activities of its members, the maximum fine is set at 10% of the sum of the total turnover of each member active on the market affected by that infringement (European Commission, 2006[27]). The French Guidelines set the maximum cap at 10% of the highest global turnover, before taxes, achieved during one of the closed financial years since the financial year preceding the one in which the practices were carried out. Fines for associations of undertakings should not exceed 10% of its highest global turnover, before taxes, achieved during one of the closed financial years since the financial year preceding the one in which the practices were carried out. Nevertheless, where infringements relate to the activities of its members, the fine should not exceed 10% of the sum of the total global turnover of each member active on the market affected by that infringement (Autorité de la concurrence, 2021, p. 13[29]).

According to the Kenyan Guidelines, the statutory limit is fixed at 10% of the firm's annual gross turnover during the firm's preceding financial year (Competition Authority of Kenya, 2020, p. 10[30]), while in the South African Guidelines it is set at 10% of the firm's annual turnover in South African and its exports from the country in the financial year preceding that in which the fine is imposed (Competition Commission of South Africa, 2015, p. 15[28]).

Inability to pay

All guidelines also affirm that the competition authority may consider, in exceptional circumstances, the firm's inability to pay when setting the fine.

Most guidelines require the firm to provide the competition authority with objective evidence that imposing a fine following the established methodology would irrevocably jeopardise the financial sustainability of the firm and result in a complete loss of value for its assets.

The Kenyan Guidelines mention that the firm's ability to pay can be considered only to allow undertakings to pay fines in reasonable instalments (Competition Authority of Kenya, 2020, p. 10[30]).

Leniency and settlement

All guidelines include guidance on leniency and/or settlement, albeit through different approaches.

For example, the European Commission Guidelines provide that the competition authorities should consider as mitigating circumstance whether the undertaking concerned has effectively co-operated outside the scope of the Leniency Notice and beyond its legal obligation to do so (European Commission, 2006[27]). The French guidelines indicate that, when setting the fines, the *Autorité de la concurrence* must consider the total or partial immunity arising from leniency (Autorité de la concurrence, 2021, pp. 13-14[29]).

Both the Kenyan and South African guidelines refer to settlements, through which the competition authority may offer a discount to the fine to be imposed on a market player for violating competition law. The Kenyan Guidelines only mention that the competition authority may, at any time during or after an investigation, enter into an agreement of settlement with the parties concerned, which may include an amount as a pecuniary penalty (Competition Authority of Kenya, 2020, p. 11[30]).

In its turn, the South African Guidelines state that the competition authority "at its sole discretion, may offer a discount of between 10% - 50% off the administrative penalty" arising from the general methodology. The following elements should be considered: (i) the timing of the settlement (i.e. firms settling in the early stages of the investigation should enjoy a greater discount than those settling in latter stages) and (ii) the extent of co-operation in the prosecution of other firms involved in the infringement (i.e. whether the firm provide timely, complete and accurate information that will corroborate other evidence at the disposal of the competition authority) (Competition Commission of South Africa, 2015, pp. 15-16[28]).

5.2.3. Less common but helpful features of guidelines reviewed

The review revealed less common but helpful features in the guidelines in the selected jurisdictions which are worth mentioning. A summary of these features is set out in Table 5.3.

Table 5.3. Less common but helpful features of fining methodology guidelines

Jurisdiction	Legally non-binding nature of guidelines	Terminology	Rights of defence	Parental liability
		OECD countries		
European Union	Implied			
France	Implied		✓	
		Non-OECD countries		
Kenya	Implied			
South Africa	✓	✓		✓

Legally non-binding nature of guidelines

Like merger and leniency programme guidelines, some fining methodology guidelines refer to their legally non-binding nature on courts, although in some of them this is only implicitly stated.

For instance, the South African Guidelines affirm that they "are not binding on the Commission, the Tribunal or the CAC in the exercise of their respective discretion, or their interpretation of the Act" (Competition Commission of South Africa, 2015, pp. 6-7[28]).

In Kenya, the non-binding nature of the guidelines is implied when they indicate that "the guidelines is not a substitute of the Act and they shall be read together with the Act and subsidiary rules made pursuant thereto" (Competition Authority of Kenya, 2020, p. 2[30]).

The French Guidelines indicate that they commit the *Autorité de la concurrence,* which seeks to refer to a consistent method to set fines. Nevertheless, it is established that the *Autorité de la concurrence* can deviate from the guidelines in light of the specific circumstances of the case (notably considering the characteristics of the practices at stake, the activities of the parties involved and the economic and legal context of the case) or for reasons of public interest (Autorité de la concurrence, 2021, p. 13[29]). The European Commission Guidelines have a similar provision (European Commission, 2006[27]).

Terminology

Also like the other categories of guidelines assessed in this report, setting methodology guidelines can present the definitions of key concepts, in order to increase understanding of the public. For instance, this is the case of the South African Guidelines, which have a section with a glossary of relevant terms (Competition Commission of South Africa, 2015, pp. 4-5[28]).

Rights of defence

The French Guidelines include procedural rules, highlighting that the competition authority should provide the investigated parties with the facts and legal basis that may impact on the setting of fines, enabling them to exercise their rights of defence (Autorité de la concurrence, 2021, p. 6[29]).

Parental liability

The South African Guidelines include rules on parental liability, specifying that parent companies not directly involved in the infringement may be held liable for an infringement where its subsidiary has violated competition law. When establishing whether the parent company is held liable, the Competition Commission should take into account whether it: (i) wholly owned the subsidiary; (ii) directly controls the subsidiary or has a decisive or material influence over the commercial policy of the subsidiary; (iii) had knowledge of the subsidiary's participation in the infringement; or (iv) derived substantial benefit from the activities of the subsidiary (Competition Commission of South Africa, 2015, pp. 17-19[28]).

Key takeaways – Fining methodology

- Fines play key a role in deterrence by making unlawful conduct less profitable. Adopting public rules or guidelines about the setting of pecuniary penalties may enhance general deterrence by allowing companies to understand how heavy the sanctions to which they may be subject are.
- The Tunisian competition law framework regarding fines is overall in line with international standards. However, there is no established fining methodology.
- Adopting guidelines about the setting of pecuniary penalties can help the Tunisian competition authorities to ensure a consistent fining policy.
- Developing fining guidelines should take several elements into account, including the objectives, the methodology, the gravity and duration of the infringement as well as the potential firm's inability to pay.

6 Leniency programme

While leniency programmes can be a powerful instrument to detect cartels and support competition enforcement, jurisdictions must provide the adequate incentives for companies to apply for leniency, including a high risk of detection and dissuasive sanctions. The Tunisian competition law follows international standards regarding leniency programmes, but no application has ever been submitted to date. Adopting leniency guidelines can help Tunisia to make its leniency programme more effective. This section presents an overview of leniency programme guidelines in selected jurisdictions, aiming to help Tunisian authorities to implement their own guidelines.

6.1. Overview of leniency regime in Tunisia

A leniency programme was established in Tunisia in 2003. Act 2015-36, particularly Article 26, updated the legal framework and currently governs the topic, which covers cartels and any type of anti-competitive agreement. In addition, Government Decree No. 2017-252 of 8 February 2017 was issued to detail the procedures for leniency applications. However, the Tunisian competition authorities have not received any leniency application to date.

Firms' incentives to apply for leniency rely on their perception of the threat of being caught and heavily sanctioned (OECD, 2023, p. 14[31]). For leniency programme to work, there must be a high risk of detection and significant sanctions, which does not seem the case in Tunisia. As indicated in the Peer Review, anti-cartel enforcement activities in Tunisia are still low, and some cartel decisions were handed without a fine being imposed, significantly reducing their deterrent effect (OECD, 2022, pp. 71-73, 91-92[1]).

Therefore, changes in the regulatory framework alone will not ensure that leniency programme will be effective. Improving the leniency programme should be carried out in parallel with more enforcement decisions and higher sanctions. Thus, it is necessary that Tunisian authorities also engage further in pro-active detection methods, including the use of economics (e.g. collusion factors, industry studies and market screening), use of information from past cases (also from other jurisdictions), industry monitoring (e.g. press and internet, career tracking of industry managers and regular contact with industry representatives), co-operation between agencies (national or foreign competition authorities or other agencies) and technology-led screens (e.g. structural screens and behavioural screens) (OECD, 2023[31]).

Figure 6.1. Total Leniency applications for the period 2015-2022 against the age of the leniency programme, by region

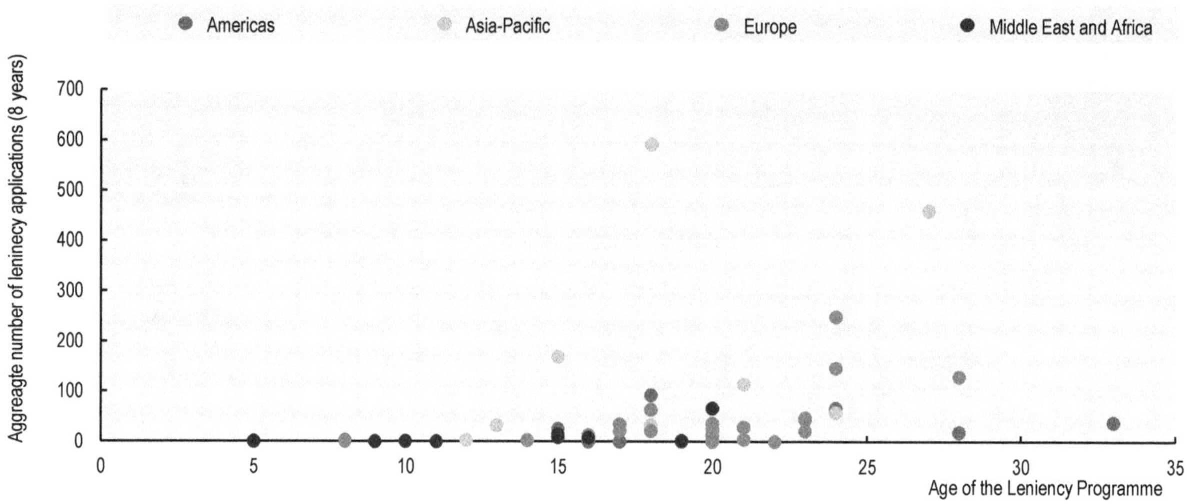

Note: Data based on the 54 jurisdictions in the OECD CompStats database that provided comparable data for all eight years and have a leniency programme.
Source: OECD CompStats database

Leniency programmes may take some time to become effective and established. Evidence from the OECD CompStats database show that there is a positive correlation between the number of leniency applications and the age of the leniency programme. Figure 6.1 illustrates this correlation suggesting the rather unusual situation of the Tunisian leniency programme that has 20 years of existence. Despite having the oldest programme in the Middle East and Africa region, Tunisia – with no application so far – performs well below the regional average of twelve leniency applications per year recorded over the 2015-2022 period (OECD, 2023[32]).

Generally speaking, Tunisia follows international standards regarding leniency programmes. For instance, leniency can ensure total or partial immunity from sanctions, depending on the applicant's position in relation to other applicants and on whether the competition authority is already aware of the infringement. Government Decree No. 2017-252 also introduced some procedural elements, in line with the practices of other jurisdictions. These include how the application can be submitted (in writing or orally), the information that must be presented and the possibility to request a marker.

In addition to provide the right incentives (e.g. pro-active detection tools and dissuasive fines), the success of a leniency programme relies on transparency and predictability. Indeed, transparency enables firms to anticipate the benefits of coming forward. Likewise, companies must be aware of the existence and the features of the leniency programme, particularly on what they may expect in return for their co-operation (OECD, 2023, p. 23[31]). In this regard, the OECD Recommendation concerning Effective Action against Hard Core Cartels assert that, to ensure effective leniency programmes, jurisdictions must provide clarity on the rules and procedures governing leniency programmes and the related benefits, as well as establish clear standards for the type and quality of information that qualifies for leniency (OECD, 2019[33]).

Article 1 of Government Decree No. 2017-252 provides that leniency applications can be submitted to either to the competition department within the Ministry of Trade or to the general rapporteur of the Competition Council. This raises significant concerns on whether confidentiality can be ensured, which is a key element of successful leniency programmes, as mentioned above. For instance, jurisdictions usually indicate specific point of contact that interested parties should approach to submit a leniency application.

The uncertainty on confidentiality is even worse since neither Act 2015-36 nor Government Decree No. 2017-252 have provisions in this regard.

Moreover, Article 26 of Act 2015-36 states that before granting leniency, the Competition Council must consult the government Commissioner. This calls into question the independence of the Competition Council to enforce its leniency programme.

The procedures introduced by Government Decree No. 2017-252 are also limited and do not cover all the main aspects of leniency applications, as highlighted below. Once again, clarity on benefits, requirements and procedures are crucial for well-functioning leniency programmes.

6.2. Leniency programme guidelines

Leniency programmes guidelines can be an effective instrument for providing transparency and predictability, increasing incentives for businesses to apply for a leniency programme. For instance, such guidelines may outline the benefits, the requirements and the procedure for a leniency application.

This section considers the elements commonly covered in leniency programme guidelines by comparing guidelines published in the selected jurisdictions, which can be used by Tunisian competition authorities when developing their own leniency guidelines.

6.2.1. Overview of guidelines reviewed

The project team has assessed the leniency programme guidelines of the selected jurisdictions, listed in Table A A.3 and summarised in Table 6.1.

Table 6.1. Overview of guidelines reviewed

Jurisdiction	Guidelines	Date of guidelines
	OECD countries	
Belgium	✓	2022
Canada	✓	2019
European Union	✓	2022
France	✓	2015
	Non-OECD countries	
Kenya	✓	2017
Philippines	✓	2019
South Africa	✓	2008

6.2.2. Common features of guidelines reviewed

The following elements have been included in the guidelines of the selected jurisdictions, as summarised in Table 6.2.

Table 6.2. Summary of common features in leniency programme guidelines in selected jurisdictions

Jurisdiction	Introductory statements	Violations covered	Eligibility criteria	Conditions	Benefits	Procedure	Confidentiality
			OECD countries				
Belgium	✓	✓	✓	✓	✓	✓	✓
Canada*	✓	✓	✓	✓	✓	✓	✓
European Union	✓	✓	✓	✓	✓	✓	✓
France	✓	✓	✓	✓	✓	✓	✓
			Non-OECD countries				
Kenya	✓	✓	✓	✓	✓	✓	✓
Philippines	✓	✓	✓	✓	✓	✓	✓
South Africa	✓	✓	✓	✓	✓	✓	✓

Note: * Canada differentiates between immunity and leniency, the latter referring to full immunity and the former to partial immunity (i.e. reduction in sanctions).

Introductory statements

Most guidelines start by introductory remarks, usually explaining the objectives of the guidelines, how they have been developed and/or the importance of leniency programmes.

For instance, the European Commission Guidelines state that they aim at clarifying "certain concepts and current practices when the Commission applies the Leniency Notice in order to ensure a high degree of transparency and predictability", as well as to "increase awareness of the additional protections and benefits enjoyed by leniency applicants, beyond the ones described in the Leniency Notice" (European Commission, 2022[34]).

In its introduction, the Belgian Guidelines describe what the leniency programme is and its legal framework, also highlighting that the Guidelines seek to provide legal certainty to the individuals and companies concerned (Autorité belge de la Concurrence, 2020[35]). The French Guidelines starts by presenting the legal framework of the leniency programme and the previous guidelines adopted in this regard, as well as describing the process of the most recent review that led to the current Guidelines (Autorité de la concurrence, 2015[36]).

The Kenyan Guidelines indicate that they were elaborated to "inform parties (…), legal practitioners, and the general public on how the Authority will handle application for leniency" (Competition Authority of Kenya, 2017[37]). Likewise, the Philippine Guidelines provides that they "serve to aid the public in understanding the concept of leniency, and to provide a transparent process in applying for the benefits offered under the program" (Philippine Competition Commission, 2019[38]).

The introductory part may also include an explanation of the rationale for the leniency programme. For instance, the Canadian Guidelines recognise the importance of leniency to uncover and stop anti-competitive activity and to deter others from engaging in similar behaviour (Competition Bureau, 2019[39]).

Violations covered by the leniency programme

All guidelines assessed expressly indicate to which competition infringements the leniency programme applies. While most leniency programme applies only to hard-core cartels, some guidelines also cover other infringements.

For instance, the Canadian Guidelines assert that immunity also applies to deceptive marketing offences (Competition Bureau, 2019, p. 7[39]). According to the European Commission Guidelines, leniency can also involve less traditional cartels, including practices such as discussion of price-setting factors on weekly reference prices, exchanges of precise information on trading positions and attempts to influence benchmark interest rates, buyer cartels and co-ordination to restrict competition on technical development

(European Commission, 2022, pp. 1-2[34]). The French Guidelines state that besides hard-core cartels the leniency programme also applies to any other similar anti-competitive behaviour among competitors, particularly co-ordinated practices established through actors in a vertical relationship (hub and spoke arrangements) (Autorité de la concurrence, 2015, p. 2[36]).

Who can benefit from the leniency programme (eligibility criteria)

Most guidelines indicate who can apply for leniency, which usually is the undertakings or associations of undertakings involved in a cartel (as long as they fulfil certain conditions, as mentioned below). Some guidelines provide that individuals involved in a cartel can also apply for leniency, such as in Belgium, Canada and the Philippines. The Kenyan Guidelines establish that leniency may also cover the applicant's directors and employees, but they are not clear whether individuals themselves can apply for leniency (Competition Authority of Kenya, 2017, p. 3[37]). The South African and European Commission guidelines indicate that individuals cannot apply for leniency, but they can be qualified as whistle blowers. However, the European Commission Guidelines clarify that EU Member States have to ensure that employees of immunity applicants of national competition authorities and the Commission are protected from sanctions at Member State level, provided that they co-operate with the relevant authorities (European Commission, 2022, p. 12[34]).

The European Commission guidelines also state that facilitators (i.e. "an undertaking that was not active on the cartelised market but which otherwise actively aided the objectives of the infringement") can apply for leniency (European Commission, 2022, p. 3[34]).

Moreover, most guidelines indicate that market players that have coerced other undertakings to join or remain in the cartel are not eligible for full immunity (Belgium, Canada, EC, France and the Philippines), although they can still benefit of reduction of fines. The Philippine Guidelines further point out that the leader in or the originator of the anti-competitive practice is also not eligible for applying for full immunity (Philippine Competition Commission, 2019, p. 21[38]). The Kenyan Guidelines provide that the leniency applicant must not have coerced others or instigated others to operationalise the agreement, suggesting that this also include partial leniency (Competition Authority of Kenya, 2017, p. 4[37]).

Conditions

All guidelines establish which are the conditions that an applicant must meet to qualify for leniency. The following elements are present in all selected guidelines: (i) the applicant must end its involvement in the cartel immediately following its application (unless otherwise requested by the competition authority, when necessary to ensure the integrity of the investigation); (ii) the applicant must ensure full and expeditious co-operation to the competition authority concerning the reported anti-competitive practices, which include providing all information and evidence of which it is aware or becomes aware and respond promptly to the competition authority requests; (iii) the applicant must not destroy, falsify or conceal information or evidence related to the reported infringement; (iv) the applicant must not disclose its application and its content (unless otherwise agreed with the competition authority).

In addition to these general conditions, specific requirements must be fulfilled for an applicant to obtain full or partial immunity (see below).

Benefits from the leniency programme

As mentioned above, according to the OECD Recommendation concerning Effective Action against Hard Core Cartels, an effective leniency programme relies on the establishment of clear benefits for applicants (OECD, 2019[33]). Accordingly, all guidelines specify what are the benefits that leniency applicants can obtain if they comply with all conditions.

Most guidelines provide for full immunity from any sanctions or reduction in sanctions, depending on the applicant's position in relation to other applicants and on whether the competition authority is already aware of the infringement. Full immunity is usually granted to the first entity that discloses its participation in a cartel and provide the competition authority information and evidence when the authority is unaware of the anti-competitive practice or, when the authority is aware of the offence, it has insufficient evidence to prosecute the cartel.

Some of guidelines (e.g. from Canada, the European Commission, France, Kenya and the Philippines) state that full immunity protects employees of leniency companies in criminal prosecutions, while the Belgian Guidelines are silent in this regard. On the other hand, the South African guidelines expressly indicate that full immunity does not protect the leniency applicant from criminal liability resulting from its participation in a cartel infringement (Competition Commission of South Africa, 2008, p. 5[40]).[10]

Most of guidelines also provide for partial immunity (i.e. a reduction in penalty) when the leniency applicants are not qualified for full immunity but contribute with additional evidence. Leniency guidelines usually set "leniency bands" with different reduction ranges, taking into account the time of application and the added value represented by the additional evidence presented. For example, this is the case of the guidelines from Belgium, the European Commission, France, Kenya and the Philippines. The Canadian guidelines establish a single band, i.e. a maximum reduction of 50% (Competition Bureau, 2019, p. 30[39]).

According to the South African guidelines, the leniency programme only benefits the "first to the door", although partial immunity can be granted to subsequent applicants through other tools (Competition Commission of South Africa, 2008, p. 5[40]).

Procedure

All guidelines provide information on the procedure to be followed during a leniency application. The steps of the leniency procedure are similar across all guidelines, including initial contact, the marker request, the submission of an application, the grant of conditional leniency and the final decision.

All guidelines highlight that applicants can informally contact the competition authority without disclosing their identity to obtain general information and clarity about the leniency programme (e.g. whether it applies to a specific behaviour).

Some guidelines (e.g. Belgium, Canada, the European Commission and the Philippines) also indicate the possibility of making a hypothetical application to establish whether leniency is available for the specific cartel the potential applicant is involved in. For this purpose, the potential applicant must provide the competition authority with the products concerned, the geographic scope and the duration of the infringement, but it is not required to disclose its identity.

In addition, all guidelines establish the possibility to request a marker, which protects the applicant's place in the line of applications with respect to a specific infringement, allowing it to gather the necessary information and evidence to qualify for leniency during a period. While most guidelines state that the competition authority will determine the period to perfect the application on a case-by-case basis, others set a more or less precise period.[11]

All guidelines also mention that the leniency applicant must present to the competition authority the relevant information and evidence at its disposal, although some guidelines provide more details in this regard. For example, the Belgian Guidelines indicate that the application must submit a leniency statement with the following information: (i) the name and address of the applicant, as well as the names and positions of the individuals within the applicant who were involved in the cartel; (ii) the name and address of other undertakings, association of undertakings or individuals involved in the cartel; (iii) products or services involved; (iii) geographic scope; (iv) duration; (v) estimate of the market volume; (vi) locations and times at which exchanges related to the cartel took place, along with content of these exchanges and the participants; (vii) the nature of the cartel; (viii) any relevant explanations concerning the provided evidence; (ix) information about any leniency applications related to the cartel in other jurisdictions; and (x) the evidence supporting these elements (Autorité belge de la Concurrence, 2020, p. 7[35]). Moreover, the

Philippine Guidelines exemplify evidence that may be relevant, such as emails, letters and minutes of meetings (Philippine Competition Commission, 2019, p. 12[38]).

Applications can usually be made in writing or orally. Oral applications are commonly transcribed by the competition authority. Only the Philippine guidelines do not mention oral applications. The guidelines are also clear regarding the point of contact in the competition authority (usually a specific position), which is relevant to ensure confidentiality.

After receiving the leniency application, the competition authority assesses the request and grants interim or conditional leniency if all conditions are met. At the end of the process, if the applicant has complied with all required conditions, the conditional leniency is converted into final leniency. Conditional leniency can be revoked if the applicant violates its obligations.

Confidentiality

All guidelines contain provisions related to confidentiality, which is an important feature required to ensure the success of leniency programmes. Indeed, according to the OECD Recommendation concerning Effective Action against Hard Core Cartels, jurisdictions should provide appropriate confidentiality protection to leniency applicants (OECD, 2019[33]), in order to guarantee the right balance between public and private enforcement and preserve the incentives to apply for leniency (OECD, 2023, p. 15[31]).

Nevertheless, the scope of confidentiality varies substantially across guidelines. Some of them are more proscriptive, clearly referring that leniency documents are protected from the complainant and interested parties.

According to the Belgian Guidelines, for example, the complainant and interest third parties do not have access to leniency applications, annexes and decisions. Other investigated parties can only have access to leniency documents to exercise their rights of defence (Autorité belge de la Concurrence, 2020, p. 10[35]).

According to the European Commission Guidelines, leniency submissions (i.e. applications and corporate statements) are protected from disclosure in civil litigation, including discovery, through the use of e-Leniency (an online platform developed by the Commission). Moreover, the Guidelines also state that the Commission expects leniency applicants to provide a full waiver of confidentiality for allowing the Commission to share leniency documents with other competition authorities (European Commission, 2022, pp. 6, 15[34]).

The Kenyan Guidelines affirm that the identity of the leniency applicant is kept confidential during the investigation and also after a decision is taken. They also indicate that any leniency applicant may request for confidentiality of the whole or any part of the material provided to the competition authority (Competition Authority of Kenya, 2017, pp. 6-7[37]).

On the other hand, other guidelines are broader and less detailed. For example, the French Guidelines are not very precise, only indicating that the *Autorité de la concurrence* preserves, within the limits of its national and EU obligations, the confidentiality of the leniency applicants' identity during the procedure until the sending of the statement of objections (Autorité de la concurrence, 2015, p. 9[36]).

Furthermore, the South African Guidelines provide that the Competition Commission shall ensure confidentiality on all information, evidence and documents submitted by the lenient applicants throughout the process. Disclosure of any information provided by the leniency applicants prior to immunity being granted depends on the consent of the applicants (Competition Commission of South Africa, 2008[40]).

According to the Philippine Guidelines, the identity of the leniency applicants is confidential and is not disclosed unless the PCC decides that their testimony or sworn statement is required for the administrative or civil case filed by the competition authority (Philippine Competition Commission, 2019, p. 24[38]).

In Canada, the leniency Guidelines provides that the identity of immunity or leniency applicants or any information provided by them are treated as confidential by the Competition Bureau. However, the guidelines list some exceptions to the confidentiality, including when disclosure is required by law or is necessary to obtain or maintain the validity of a judicial authorisation for the exercise of investigative powers, as well as when the party has agreed to disclosure (Competition Bureau, 2019, pp. 41-42[39]).

6.2.3. Less common but helpful features of guidelines reviewed

The review revealed less common but helpful features in the guidelines in the selected jurisdictions which are worth mentioning. A summary of these features is set out in Table 6.3.

Table 6.3. Less common but helpful features of leniency programme guidelines

Jurisdiction	Legally non-binding nature	Terminology	Consequences for civil liability	Checklist and template documents
		OECD countries		
Belgium		✓		
Canada	✓	✓*	Implied	✓
European Union	✓		✓	
France			✓	
		Non-OECD countries		
Kenya		✓		
Philippines	Implied		✓	
South Africa			✓	

Note: * The Canadian Guidelines do not include a glossary, but clarify some terms in the introduction.

Legally non-binding nature of guidelines

Like merger guidelines, competition authorities may also wish to expressly indicate that the leniency guidelines are legally not binding on courts, even if this is implied in some jurisdictions.

For instance, Canadian Guidelines indicate that they "do not provide legal advice" (Competition Bureau, 2019, p. 7[39]). Likewise, the European Commission Guidelines specify that they "are not intended to constitute a statement of the law and they are without prejudice to the interpretation of Article 101 and the Leniency Notice by the European Courts" (European Commission, 2022, p. 1[34]).

The Philippine Guidelines state that the Guidelines are "not a substitute for the PCA [Philippine Competition Act] and the Leniency Rules" (Philippine Competition Commission, 2019, p. 3[38]).

Terminology

Certain guidelines, such as in Belgium and Kenya, include a glossary with the definition of key technical terms, which can help enhance understanding of the leniency programme. A glossary can be particularly useful in jurisdictions where leniency is new or less effective.

While not having a formal glossary, the Canadian Guidelines explain the meaning of some terms, such as "party", "immunity applicant" and "lenient applicant" (Competition Bureau, 2019, p. 7[39]).

Consequences for civil liability

Some guidelines mention the consequences of leniency for civil liability. A few guidelines (e.g. France and South Africa) specify that immunity granted through leniency does not protect the applicant from civil liability resulting from its participation in a cartel.

The European Guidelines explain that the leniency programme protects applicants against exposure to civil damages. In particular, immunity recipients are only jointly and severally liable to their direct and indirect customers and to other cartel victims if full compensation cannot be obtained from the other cartelists (European Commission, 2022, p. 12[34]).

On the other hand, the Philippine Guidelines indicate that civil actions initiated by the PCC on behalf of affected parties and third parties may be avoided or reduced through the leniency programme (Philippine Competition Commission, 2019, p. 8[38]).

The Canadian Guidelines do not expressly mention that applicants are not protected from civil damages actions, but they state that the Competition Bureau has no interest in penalising applicants for early disclosure or co-operation in a civil action (Competition Bureau, 2019, p. 43[39]).

Checklist and template documents

The Canadian Guidelines provide for a checklist to guide applicants as regards the information that they must provide to the competition authority. For instance, this refers to the parties, the product, the industry, the market, the conduct and its impact. The Canadian guidelines also include some template documents, which may be useful for helping leniency applications and providing further transparency to potential leniency applicants.

Key takeaways – Leniency programme

- While leniency programmes can be a powerful instrument to detect cartels and support competition enforcement, jurisdictions must provide the adequate incentives for companies to apply for leniency, including a high risk of detection and dissuasive sanctions.
- Transparency and predictability are crucial for a successful leniency programme.
- The Tunisian competition law follows international standards regarding leniency programmes, but no application has ever been submitted to date.
- Adopting leniency guidelines can help Tunisia to make its leniency programme more effective.
- When developing leniency guidelines, several elements should be taken into account, including who is the point of contact in the competition authority that interested parties should approach to submit an application, the possibility to request a marker and the information and evidence that should be presented.

7 Compliance programme

Competition compliance programmes are not common in Tunisia. Developing guidelines about compliance programmes can help the Tunisian competition authorities to promote and incentivise the adoption of such programmes. This section presents an overview of compliance programme guidelines in selected jurisdictions, aiming to help Tunisian authorities to implement their own guidelines.

7.1. Overview of compliance programme in Tunisia

According to the Peer Review, competition compliance programmes are not common in Tunisia, regardless of the size of the firm (OECD, 2022, p. 151[1]). Tunisian competition authorities could help encouraging the adoption of such programmes, for instance by issuing guidelines in this regard. However, the lack of clear roles and tasks allocation between the DGCEE and the Competition Council when it comes to competition advocacy might pose a challenge in this regard.

Competition authorities have increasingly engaged in preventive compliance efforts worldwide, for instance by promoting compliance programmes. These efforts are complemented by several initiatives, including the ICC Antitrust Compliance Toolkit (ICC, 2013[41]). Compliance programmes include online information and seminars on competition law for employees to help them identify potential anti-competitive practices and the procedures to follow if a potential breach is found.

To promote the adoption of compliance programmes that avoid and/or detect breaches, it is important to develop a strategy and clarify the approach to incentivise firms to adopt them. This includes deciding on whether the authorities should reward companies for adopting a compliance programme, for example by reducing fines for infringements.

> *Whether or not a benefit is granted in return for the existence of a compliance programme does not depend on the region in which a jurisdiction is located. In Asia, many jurisdictions are willing to grant reduced fines, and the Association of Southeast Asian Nations (ASEAN) guidelines suggest that a reduction in fines could provide an incentive for companies to introduce or improve these programmes. Some Latin American countries have developed compliance policies, and Brazil, Chile, and Peru grant a reduced fine if the criteria set out in their guidelines are met. Similarly, some European jurisdictions are willing to grant a reduction in fines. In North America, the landscape has changed fundamentally since 2011, with Canada and the United States now making clear their willingness to consider compliance programmes (OECD, 2021[42]).*

Many jurisdictions have invested significantly in guidance on compliance programmes. Guidelines typically indicate the main elements of an effective compliance programme, resting on the premise that they need to be adjusted to the specificities of firms, their main compliance risks and over time (OECD, 2021[42]).

7.2. Compliance programme guidelines

This section considers the elements commonly covered in compliance programme guidelines by comparing guidelines published in the selected jurisdictions, which can be used by Tunisian competition authorities when developing their own compliance programme guidelines.

7.2.1. Overview of guidelines reviewed

The project team has assessed the compliance programme guidelines of selected jurisdictions, listed in Table A A.5 and summarised in Table 7.1.

Table 7.1. Overview of guidelines reviewed

Jurisdiction	Guidelines	Date of guidelines
	OECD countries	
Belgium	✓*	2016
Canada	✓	2015
European Union	✓	2012
France	✓	2022
	Non-OECD countries	
Kenya	-	-
Philippines	-	-
South Africa	-	-

Note: * Belgium has not properly developed guidelines on compliance programmes, but the competition authority has included a chapter on the topic in its Guidelines on Competition Law to SMEs.

7.2.2. Common features of guidelines reviewed

The following elements have been included in the guidelines of the selected jurisdictions, as summarised in Table 7.2.

Table 7.2. Summary of common features in compliance programme guidelines in selected jurisdictions

Jurisdiction	Benefits	No one-size-fits-all approach	Management commitment	Risk assessment	Transparency, communication and documentation	Training	Reporting	Monitoring	Regular evaluation and update
					OECD countries				
Belgium	✓	✓	✓	✓	✓	✓	✓		
Canada	✓	✓	✓	✓	✓	✓	✓	✓	✓
European Union	✓	✓	✓	✓	✓	✓	✓	✓	✓
France	✓	✓	✓	✓	✓	✓	✓	✓	✓

Benefits of compliance programme

All guidelines refer to the benefits of implementing a compliance programme, both to the firm at stake and the whole economy. Indeed, compliance programmes aim to increase prevention, detection and deterrence of competition infringements.

For example, the Canadian Guidelines state that compliance programmes aim at (i) informing business of how to minimise competition infringements, avoiding the likely penalties and the costs associated in defending against competition law enforcement; (ii) detecting at an early stage behaviours that may contravene competition law, allowing the firm to be the first-in to request immunity or to be better placed to apply for leniency; and (iii) identifying circumstances where the company is potentially affected by the anti-competitive behaviour of other parties. Other benefits are also mentioned, including maintaining a good reputation and improving a business' ability to attract and retain customers and suppliers who value companies that operate ethically (Competition Bureau, 2010, pp. 3-4[43]).

In addition, according to the French Guidelines, competition compliance programmes have three main benefits: (i) help establish free and undistorted competition; (ii) assist preventing financial and reputational risks; and (iii) facilitate the detection of infringements (Autorité de la concurrence, 2022, pp. 3-4[44]).

The guidelines of the European Commission mention that firms should comply with competition rules not only for being regarded as doing business ethically, but also for avoiding the potentially high cost of non-compliance (European Commission, 2012, p. 9[45]).

As for the impact of compliance programmes on fines imposed in case of competition infringements, the guidelines reviewed are not uniform. On the one hand, the Canadian Guidelines state that the existence of a programme will be treated as a mitigating factor by the Competition Bureau (Competition Bureau, 2010, p. 6[43]). On the other hand, the Belgian Guidelines provide that compliance programmes are not considered a mitigating circumstance in case of infringement (Autorité belge de la concurrence, 2016, p. 14[46]). Likewise, the European Commission Guidelines specify that the existence of a compliance programme is neither considered an aggravating nor a mitigating circumstance for the purpose of setting fines (European Commission, 2012, p. 21[45]). The French guidelines are silent in this regard.[12]

No one-size-fits-all approach

All guidelines highlight that there is no one-size-fits-all approach to compliance programmes, meaning that firms should implement different programmes, for instance as regards their size, sector of activity and the risks they face in their day-to-day operations.

For example, the Canadian Guidelines state that "the Bureau recognizes that SMEs and larger business have different needs and concerns", and therefore "each business should implement and follow a corporate compliance programme that is commensurate with its size and business activities" (Competition Bureau, 2010, p. 1[43]).

Likewise, the European Commission Guidelines mention that compliances programmes should be tailor-made to the company concerned, considering its needs, as well as its type, size and resources (European Commission, 2012, p. 21[45]).

The French Guidelines also establish that compliance programmes should be "designed by and for the company; it is a 'tailor-made' project that must be adapted to the markets, activities and products, internal organisation and culture, as well as to the decision-making chain and the mode of governance" (Autorité de la concurrence, 2022, p. 5[44]).

Management commitment

Most guidelines state that an effective compliance programme requires the full, visible support of the firm's leadership. This should be reflected by the resources committed to the programme, including the appointment of the compliance officer.

For instance, the Canadian Guidelines stress the importance of management's clear, continuous and unequivocal commitment and support. They also recommend that a firm assign responsibility for its compliance programme (the compliance officer) to a high-level executive position, who should be appointed by the board of directors (Competition Bureau, 2010, pp. 10-12[43]).

The European Commission Guidelines indicate that "unequivocal senior management support is vital" for effective compliance programmes. They also suggest the designation of an individual member of the senior management as the compliance officer to guarantee lasting commitment to and visibility for compliance. Moreover, firms must devote sufficient resources, vis-à-vis their size and the risks they face, to ensure the existence of a credible compliance programme (European Commission, 2012, p. 17[45]).

The French Guidelines also refer to the importance of management leadership for "involving all teams and leading the company to effectively commit to compliance" (Autorité de la concurrence, 2022, p. 6[44]).

The Belgian Guidelines mention that the responsible for the compliance programme should have access to the shareholders (owners) and top management of your company and regularly reports to them (Autorité belge de la concurrence, 2016, p. 16[46]).

Risk assessment

The guidelines reviewed in this report also state that companies must regularly identify and assess their compliance risks, particularly when entering new markets or hiring for key staff. In particular, they should identify operations, units and personnel most at risk.

The Belgian Guidelines, for example, suggest that companies assess their risks, including whether they hold a dominant position in a relevant market, as well as whether the most important arrangements (e.g. distribution contracts and potential joint venture agreements or structural collaboration agreements, notably with competitors) involve hard-core restrictions (Autorité belge de la concurrence, 2016, p. 15[46]).

Furthermore, according to the Canadian Guidelines, companies must engage regularly in a risk assessment of their potential risks, in order to design proportionate compliance measures to meet those risks. Risk assessment should identify areas of risk, employees more exposed to risk and changes that can affect risk profiles (Competition Bureau, 2010, pp. 12-15[43]).

The guidelines European Commission suggest that an effective compliance programme is based on a comprehensive analysis of the areas in which the company is most likely to run a risk of violating EU competition law, in light of the sector of activity, the frequency and level of the company's interaction with competitors, the characteristics of the market, but also the position held by each member of staff (European Commission, 2012, p. 16[45]).

The French Guidelines also refer to the need for a risk analysis, "which leads to the establishment of a map of the identified risks" (Autorité de la concurrence, 2022, p. 5[44]).

Transparency, communication and documentation

All guidelines highlight that compliance programmes should be implemented in a transparent manner, properly documented and disclosed throughout the company.

The Canadian Guidelines recommend that firms develop and document compliance policies and procedures, which should be designed in line with the company's operations and the daily tasks of the employees. These policies and procedures should include internal controls designed to prevent infringements from happening (e.g. with a list of "dos" and "don'ts" and "red flag" issues). Compliance policies and procedures should be distributed to all staff or, at least, to all relevant staff. Employees should also be required to sign a certification letter stating that they have read and understand the company's Code of Conduct and applicable compliance policies (Competition Bureau, 2010, pp. 14-16[43]).

Similarly, the European Commission Guidelines indicate that the company's compliance strategy should preferably be laid down in writing (e.g. in the form a manual) and disseminated throughout its entire organizational structure. Establishing a practical set of "don'ts" and "red flags" is also encouraged. Moreover, staff might be required to provide written acknowledgment of receipt of relevant information, such as compliance manual (European Commission, 2012, pp. 16-17[45]).

The guidelines from Belgium suggest the establishment of a code of conduct taking into account what is relevant to the company at stake (Autorité belge de la concurrence, 2016, p. 16[46]). Likewise, the French

Guidelines refer to the implementation of information measures, which may contain the existence, purpose and content of the compliance programme, the meaning and practical scope of the competition rules, as well as the internal mechanisms for obtaining advice or alerting someone to the existence of an actual of potential infringement of these rules (Autorité de la concurrence, 2022, pp. 6-7[44]).

Training

According to all guidelines, compliance programmes should include mandatory compliance training for all staff in position with identified risks and to new employees.

The European Commission Guidelines point out the relevance of training on EU competition law. This can be done, for example, by including a module on competition in newcomers training program. In particular, training should be provided to staff members who are most likely to face compliance risks, such as sales personnel and sales managers and anyone attending trade associations or industry events (European Commission, 2012, p. 18[45]).

Likewise, the French Guidelines highlight the relevance of the training and awareness-raising activities on competition rules and the practical operation of the compliance programme, although different categories of personnel should receive different level of actions according to their position and their exposure to risk (Autorité de la concurrence, 2022, p. 7[44]).

The Belgian Guidelines refer to the need to provide staff with appropriate training on compliance issues, for instance as part of the starter pack (Autorité belge de la concurrence, 2016, p. 17[46]).

The Canadian Guidelines also mention the need for on-going training on compliance issues for staff at all levels who are in a position to potentially engage in, or be exposed to, competition infringement (Competition Bureau, 2010, pp. 16-18[43]).

Reporting

All guidelines acknowledge that compliance programmes should include a system to guarantee that personnel can report violations of the compliance programme or competition infringements confidentially and without threat of retaliation.

For example, the Canadian Guidelines suggest that a confidential, internal reporting procedure incentivises staff to provide timely and reliable information on potential competition violations. Accordingly, "managers, employees and other acting for the business must be able to obtain advice and raise concerns without fear of retaliation and without first having to raise issues with their superiors or supervisors". Compliance programmes should clearly indicate which actions require reporting, and when, how and to whom they should be reported (Competition Bureau, 2010, pp. 19-20[43]).

The European Commission Guidelines establish that proper internal reporting mechanisms are a feature of a successful compliance strategy. The company should create "an environment that encourages employees to speak up when they are confronted with questionable situations" (European Commission, 2012, p. 18[45]). Likewise, both the Belgian and French guidelines mention the need to introduce a procedure for handling requests for advice and alerts of actual or potential infringements (Autorité belge de la concurrence, 2016, p. 16[46]; Autorité de la concurrence, 2022, p. 7[44]).

Monitoring

Most guidelines highlight the importance of monitoring on an on-going basis how the compliance programme has been working and whether and how potential infringements have been managed.

For instance, the Canadian Guidelines state that firms should monitor their compliance programmes regularly to guarantee that their implementation is effective. In addition, they should also routinely verify whether competition infringements have occurred and whether they have been dealt with appropriately, including by co-operating with the Competition Bureau (Competition Bureau, 2010, pp. 18-20[43]).

The French Guidelines emphasise the relevance of controls to ensure that the compliance programme is being followed at all levels of the company (Autorité de la concurrence, 2022, p. 7[44]).

The European Commission Guidelines mention that monitoring and auditing are effective tools to prevent and detect anti-competitive practice inside the company. When the compliance programme cannot prevent any infringement from happening, the company must take appropriate measures without delay, so that any potential infringement is swiftly brought to an end. This includes, for instance, co-operating under the leniency programme and the settlement procedure (European Commission, 2012, pp. 18-19[45]).

Regular evaluation and update

Most guidelines also recognise that compliance programmes are a drive for continuous improvement, requiring regular review to guarantee they remain up to date and effective.

The need for regular assessment of a programme's ability to deliver its core objective is indicated by the Canadian Guidelines as a requirement for a credible and effective compliance programme. This continuous process can also capture new or emerging risks. Various tools can be used to conduct a review, such as individual and group interviews, focus groups, surveys and exit interviews. Review by an independent third party should also be considered. When necessary, changes to the compliance programme should be implemented (Competition Bureau, 2010, pp. 21-22[43]). The European Commission and French guidelines also mention that compliance programmes should be regularly reviewed and updated (European Commission, 2012, p. 18[45]; Autorité de la concurrence, 2022, p. 7[44]).

7.2.3. Less common but helpful features of guidelines reviewed

The review revealed less common but helpful features in the guidelines in the selected jurisdictions which are worth mentioning. A summary of these features is set out in Table 7.3.

Table 7.3. Less common but helpful features of compliance programme guidelines

Jurisdiction	Voluntary nature of compliance programmes	Disciplinary actions and incentives for compliance	Checklist and template documents	Examples	Reference to additional information
OECD countries					
Belgium					✓
Canada	✓	✓	✓	✓	
European Union		✓			✓
France					

Voluntary nature of compliance programmes

The Canadian Guidelines expressly indicate that the implementation of a compliance programme is generally voluntary. However, it is mentioned that in some circumstances the Bureau may recommend or request the establishment of a compliance programme and the appointment of an independent compliance monitor to oversee the implementation and operation of any such compliance programme (Competition Bureau, 2010, p. 2[43]).

Disciplinary actions and incentives for compliance

The Canadian and European Commission guidelines state that compliance programmes should introduce incentives for employers and disciplinary measures in case of breach of competition law and the compliance programme.

According to the Canadian Guidelines, compliance programmes should explicitly provide for consistent disciplinary actions (e.g. suspension, demotion, dismissal or legal action) to be taken when individuals fail to comply with the programme and/or infringe competition law. Moreover, compliance programmes should establish that disciplinary actions will be taken when a manager fails to take reasonable steps to prevent or detect competition violations or does not initiate appropriate disciplinary action. In addition, compliance programmes should provide appropriate incentives for performing in line with them, for example by considering compliance and active support of the programme for the purposes of employee evaluations, promotions and bonuses (Competition Bureau, 2010, pp. 20-21[43]).

The guidelines of the European Commission also refer to introduction of penalties for breach of the internal compliance rules, which need nevertheless be consistent with national employment law. Furthermore, the guidelines indicate the importance of implementing positive incentives for employees to consider compliance duties with utmost seriousness. For instance, this could be achieved by including compliance duties as part of job descriptions and considering vigilant attitude as the staff evaluation criteria (European Commission, 2012, p. 17[45]).

On the other hand, the Belgian guidelines state that more important than dismissing the individuals involved in competition infringements is to ensure that they co-operate as closely as possible with the investigations (Autorité belge de la concurrence, 2016, p. 16[46]).

Checklist and template documents

The Canadian guidelines include a "Due Diligence Checklist" to help businesses comply with competition law. They also provide the "Corporate Compliance Program Framework", which is a flexible tool that can be adapted to the specific activities and resources of a particular business. There is also a "Certification Letter" template, which all employees at compliance risk should be asked to adhere to (Competition Bureau, 2010, pp. 25-40[43]).

Examples

The Canadian guidelines provide for hypothetical examples to illustrate the analytical framework that the Bureau will typically apply when assessing a pre-existing competition law compliance programme (Competition Bureau, 2010, pp. 41-53[43]). Such examples can be very useful for guiding businesses when developing compliance programmes, with several practical aspects.

Reference to additional information

The Belgian and European Commission guidelines include references to other relevant documents which may guide business as regards compliance programmes. For instance, the Belgian Guidelines indicate compliance guidelines from other competition authorities or organisations (Autorité belge de la concurrence, 2016, p. 18[46]), while the European Commission refer to relevant webpages from the Commission (European Commission, 2012, p. 22[45]).

Key takeaways – Compliance programme

- Compliance programmes can contribute to an effective competition compliance policy, by helping prevent anti-competitive conduct, facilitate detection and/or reduce the duration of such behaviour.
- Competition compliance programmes are not common in Tunisia. Developing guidelines about compliance programmes can help the Tunisian competition authorities to promote and incentivise the adoption of such programmes.
- When designing their compliance programme guidelines, the Tunisian authorities should indicate the elements they consider essential for an effective competition compliance programme such as benefits, management commitments and risk assessment.

8 Recommendations

This section presents recommendations for Tunisia to improve its competition policy framework in line with well-established international best practices, particularly related to merger control, fining methodology, leniency programme and compliance programme. In addition, relevant recommendations made in the Peer Review are reiterated.

Tunisia started an ambitious programme to implement an effective competition law and policy. As highlighted in the 2022 Peer Review, the conditions for the competition entities to thrive and to make a significant contribution to achieving competitive markets in the country to the benefit of the country's consumers and businesses, and leading to increased productivity, innovation, growth and employment are partly in place.

To further improve the legal and policy framework in line with well-established international best practices, this report suggests a number of improvements to the competition enforcement and advocacy frameworks, particularly by the development of competition guidelines in four areas: merger control, fining methodology, leniency programme and compliance programme. A draft document of merger guidelines was already produced by the Tunisian competition authorities, which suggests that this should continue to be their focus in the short-term. Guidelines on fining methodology should be prioritised in a second stage, followed by guidelines on leniency and compliance programmes.

As discussed in this report, competition guidelines should follow a process that includes stakeholder consultation. Specifying the legally non-binding nature of guidelines on courts – despite their legal effects, especially on competition authorities – may also be relevant in Tunisia, where the issuance of such documents is not a common practice.

While competition guidelines can play an important role in fostering competition policy in Tunisia, this should go hand in hand with addressing specific shortcomings in the enforcement and advocacy frameworks. In this context, this report reiterates the relevant recommendations made in the Peer Review.

Based on the analysis provided in chapters 4 to 7, the following recommendations can be summarised:

8.1. Merger control

Tunisia is currently seeking to implement merger guidelines to enhance transparency, legal certainty and predictability of action by competition authorities, in line with international best practices. The current draft should consider addressing the following elements before being submitted to stakeholder consultation:

- In the absence of the implementation of the Peer Review recommendation to transfer responsibility for merger control to the Competition Council, ensure a more co-ordinated approach on the assessment of mergers between the Competition Council and the DGCEE.
- Specify how the competition assessment varies according to the nature of the transaction (i.e. horizontal or non-horizontal mergers).

- Provide further elements regarding market definition, which is particularly relevant since one of the notification thresholds is based on a market share test.
- Elaborate on the nature of the relevant economic test used for assessing mergers, in order to ensure a consistent and transparent review of transactions.
- Further detail how remedies should be set, including with more descriptive examples.
- Establish "safe harbours" to specify the cases that are not likely to raise competition concerns, possibly subject to a simplified procedure.
- Include additional examples and reference to relevant caselaw, providing more details on the substantive analysis and procedures of these cases.
- Introduce a glossary with explanations of relevant terminology.

While issuing merger guidelines can play an important role in fostering merger control in Tunisia, it should be accompanied by reforms in this area (including possible legislative changes) to address specific shortcomings, in particular:

- Implement a two-phase approach, as well as a simplified merger regime to ensure that mergers that do not raise material competitive concerns are subject to expedited review and clearance.
- Introduce merger notification forms, spelling out the required information and documents that the merging parties must submit within the merger notification.
- Review the turnover-based notification threshold and consider reducing the current numerical level, in order to ensure an efficient setting of threshold levels that reflect the reality of the Tunisian economy and guarantee a well-functioning and efficient merger control regime.
- Ensure that gun-jumping infringements are sanctioned, which is necessary to guarantee the efficiency of its merger control regime.
- Consider implementing merger filing fees, in addition to other resources already in place, in order to increase competition authorities' budget. The filing fees should be reasonable and based on one of the criteria usually adopted by other jurisdictions.

8.2. Fining methodology

The Tunisian competition law framework regarding fines is overall in line with international standards, but there is no established fining methodology. Developing such a methodology can help Tunisian competition authorities ensure a consistent fining policy. This may reduce discretion of administrative authorities when setting fines, which can be useful in judicial review, as courts can rely on an objective procedure previously established. Moreover, this would enhance transparency, legal certainty and general deterrence by allowing companies to understand how heavy the sanctions to which they may be subject are. When developing fining guidelines, the following elements should be taken into account:

- Clearly indicate the objectives of fines.
- Spell out the methodology for setting fines, including the determination of the basic amount, its adjustment according to aggravating and mitigating circumstances and statutory limits of fines.
- Consider the gravity and duration of the infringement when setting fines.
- Whether the firm's inability to pay can be taken into account and, if so, how.

While issuing fining methodology guidelines can play an important role in fostering competition enforcement and advocacy in Tunisia, it should be accompanied by reforms in this area (including possible legislative changes) to address specific shortcomings, in particular:

- Enable the imposition of adequate fines, especially in cartel cases, in order to increase deterrence of wrongdoings.

- Improve the framework conditions for the enforcement of competition law sanctions by:
    - Removing the automatic suspensive effect when an appeal is made to the Administrative Court against a Competition Council decision.
    - Granting full representation powers to the Competition Council before other public bodies, including the Administrative Court.
    - Providing the Council with the powers to oversee the implementation of its own decisions.

8.3. Leniency programme

Tunisia has adopted a leniency programme for more than two decades, but to date no applications have ever been submitted. The issuance of guidelines can be useful in further promoting the Tunisian leniency programme. In this context, the following elements should be considered in future leniency guidelines:

- Indicate the violations covered by the leniency programme.
- Establish the eligibility criteria and the conditions to apply for leniency.
- Clearly state the benefits from the leniency programme.
- Spell out the procedural aspects of a leniency application, including who is the point of contact in the competition authority that interested parties should approach to submit an application, the possibility to request a marker and the information and evidence that should be presented.
- Explain how and to what extent confidentiality of leniency applications is ensured.
- State the consequences of leniency for civil liability.
- Provide a checklist regarding the elements that must be fulfilled to ensure a complete application, as well as template documents.

In parallel with issuing guidelines, the following actions should be implemented to improve the Tunisian leniency programme:

- Ensure that wrongdoers have adequate incentives to apply for leniency, for instance by:
    - Further engaging in pro-active detection methods, including the use of economics (e.g. collusion factors, industry studies and market screening), use of information from past cases (also from other jurisdictions), industry monitoring (e.g. press and internet, career tracking of industry managers and regular contact with industry representatives), co-operation between agencies (national or foreign competition authorities or other agencies) and technology-led screens (e.g. structural screens and behavioural screens).
    - Guaranteeing that sanctions imposed on anti-competitive behaviour are sufficiently deterrent.
- Abolish the obligation for the Competition Council to consult the government Commissioner prior to enforcing the leniency programme.

8.4. Compliance programme

The development of guidelines can help encourage the adoption of competition compliance programmes in Tunisia. The following elements should be considered when developing compliance programme guidelines:

- Indicate the benefits of compliance programmes, including whether they are considered a mitigating or aggravating circumstance for the purpose of setting fines.
- Recognise that there is no one-size-fits-all approach to compliance programmes, and therefore each firm should implement its own programme taking into account its size, sector of activity and the risks it faces in its day-to-day operations.

- Highlight the importance of management commitment, risk assessment, transparency and documentation, training, reporting mechanisms, as well as regular evaluation and update.
- Provide businesses with template documents that can serve as a starting point for developing compliance programmes.
- Reach out to companies to explain their obligations under competition law and to promote the adoption of compliance programmes in all economic sectors.

The incentives for firms to develop competition compliance programmes are closely linked to the effectiveness of the competition law regime and strength of the competition authority/ies in the country. A well-functioning and robust competition authority can influence how companies perceive the importance of compliance programmes and their willingness to invest in them. In addition to guidelines on compliance programmes, the Tunisian authorities should therefore consider the following recommendations:

- Strengthen the institutional competition law framework, notably by strengthening the mandate and powers of the Competition Council and ensure its independence.
- Strengthen competition enforcement by ensuring that the competition authorities are adequately resourced to effectively and efficiently investigate and prosecute cases. This includes opening investigations and conducting dawn raids where needed, with the aim to ensure a credible deterrent effect.

References

Autorité belge de la Concurrence (2020), *Lignes directrices sur la clémence de l'Autorité belge de la Concurrence*, https://www.abc-bma.be/sites/default/files/content/download/files/20200522_clementierichtsnoeren_lignes_directrices_clemence.pdf. [35]

Autorité belge de la concurrence (2016), *Les règles de concurrence - un guide pour les PME*, https://www.abc-bma.be/sites/default/files/content/download/files/20160704_conformite_pme.pdf. [46]

Autorité de la concurrence (2022), *Framework document of 23 May 2022 on competition compliance programmes*, https://www.autoritedelaconcurrence.fr/sites/default/files/2022-06/Conformite_nouveau%20doc-cadre_VEN.pdf. [44]

Autorité de la concurrence (2021), *Communiqué de l'Autorité de la concurrence relatif à la méthode de détermination des sanctions pécuniaires*, https://www.autoritedelaconcurrence.fr/sites/default/files/Communique_sanction.pdf. [29]

Autorité de la concurrence (2020), *Merger Control Guidelines of the Autorité de la concurrence*, https://www.autoritedelaconcurrence.fr/en/article/see-autorites-new-merger-control-guidelines-english. [17]

Autorité de la concurrence (2015), *Communiqué de procédure du 3 avril 2015 relatif au programme de clémence français*, https://www.autoritedelaconcurrence.fr/sites/default/files/cpro_autorite_clemence_revise.pdf. [36]

Banet, C. (2020), "Legal Status and Legal Effects of the Commission's State Aid Guidelines: The Case of the Guidelines on State Aid for Environmental Protection and Energy (EEAG) (2014-2020)", *European State Aid Law Quarterly*. [49]

Belgian Competition Authority (2023), *Mergers*, https://www.belgiancompetition.be/en/mergers. [14]

Bulgarian Commission on Protection of Competition/UNCTAD (n.d.), *Guidelines for Implementing Competition Advocacy*, Sofia Competition Forum, https://unctad.org/meetings/en/Contribution/ccpb_SCF_AdvocacyGuidelines_en.pdf. [2]

COMESA (2014), *COMESA Merger Assessment Guidelines*, https://www.comesacompetition.org/wp-content/uploads/2014/10/141121_COMESA-Merger-Assessment-Guideline-October-31st-2014.pdf. [7]

Competition Authority of Kenya (2021), *Joint Venture Guidelines*, https://cak.go.ke/mandate/mergers/forms-guidelines. [23]

Competition Authority of Kenya (2020), *Competition Administrative Penalties and Settlement Guidelines*, https://cak.go.ke/sites/default/files/Competition%20Administrative%20Penalties%20and%20Settlement%20Guidelines.pdf. [30]

Competition Authority of Kenya (2017), *Leniency Program Guidelines*, https://cak.go.ke/sites/default/files/guidelines/enforcement-compliance/Leniency%20Programme%20Guidelines.pdf. [37]

Competition Authority of Kenya (n.d.), *Consolidated Guidelines on the Substantive Assessment of Mergers under the Competition Act*, https://cak.go.ke/mandate/mergers/forms-guidelines. [18]

Competition Bureau (2019), *Immunity and Leniency Programs under the Competition Act*, https://ised-isde.canada.ca/site/bureau-concurrence-canada/fr/comment-nous-favorisons-concurrence/education-sensibilisation/programmes-dimmunite-clemence-vertu-loi-concurrence. [39]

Competition Bureau (2011), *Enforcement Guidelines - Merger Enforcement Guidelines*, https://ised-isde.canada.ca/site/competition-bureau-canada/en/how-we-foster-competition/education-and-outreach/publications/merger-enforcement-guidelines. [16]

Competition Bureau (2010), *Corporate Compliance Programs*, https://ised-isde.canada.ca/site/competition-bureau-canada/en/how-we-foster-competition/compliance-and-enforcement/corporate-compliance-programs. [43]

Competition Bureau (2006), *Information Bulletin on Merger Remedies in Canada*, https://ised-isde.canada.ca/site/competition-bureau-canada/en/how-we-foster-competition/education-and-outreach/publications/information-bulletin-merger-remedies-canada. [19]

Competition Commission of South Africa (2015), *Guidelines for the Determination of Administrative Penalties for Prohibited Practices*, https://www.compcom.co.za/wp-content/uploads/2018/11/Final-Guidelines-for-Determination-of-Admin-Penalties-MAY-2015.pdf. [28]

Competition Commission of South Africa (2008), *Corporate Leniency Policy*, https://www.compcom.co.za/wp-content/uploads/2017/11/CLP-public-version-120520081.pdf. [40]

European Commission (2022), *Frequently Asked Questions (FAQs) on Leniency*, https://competition-policy.ec.europa.eu/system/files/2022-10/leniency_FAQs_2.pdf. [34]

European Commission (2012), *Compliance matters - What companies can do better to respect EU competition rules*, https://op.europa.eu/en/publication-detail/-/publication/78f46c48-e03e-4c36-bbbe-aa08c2514d7a/language-en. [45]

European Commission (2008), *Commission Notice on remedies acceptable under Council Regulation (EC) No 139/2004 and under Commission Regulation (EC) No 802/2004*, https://ec.europa.eu/competition/mergers/legislation/files_remedies/remedies_notice_en.pdf. [20]

European Commission (2008), *Guidelines on the assessment of horizontal mergers under the Council Regulation on the control of concentrations between undertakings*, https://eur-lex.europa.eu/legal-content/EN/ALL/?uri=celex%3A52004XC0205%2802%29. [21]

European Commission (2008), *Guidelines on the assessment of non-horizontal mergers under the Council Regulation on the control of concentrations between undertakings*, https://eur-lex.europa.eu/LexUriServ/LexUriServ.do?uri=OJ:C:2008:265:0006:0025:en:PDF. [22]

European Commission (2006), *Guidelines on the method of setting fines imposed pursuant to Article 23(2)(a) of Regulation*, https://eur-lex.europa.eu/legal-content/EN/TXT/?uri=celex%3A52006XC0901%2801%29. [27]

European Commission (2005), *Commission Notice on restrictions directly related and necessary to concentrations*, https://eur-lex.europa.eu/legal-content/EN/TXT/PDF/?uri=CELEX:52005XC0305(02)&from=EN. [25]

ICC (2013), *ICC Antitrust Compliance Toolkit*, https://2go.iccwbo.org/icc-antitrust-compliance-toolkit-english-version.html#description. [41]

ICN (2006), *ICN Merger Guidelines Workbook*, https://www.internationalcompetitionnetwork.org/wp-content/uploads/2018/05/MWG_MergerGuidelinesWorkbook.pdf. [13]

ICN (2004), *Project on Merger Guidelines*, https://www.internationalcompetitionnetwork.org/wp-content/uploads/2018/05/MWG_MergerGuidelinesReport.pdf (accessed on 21 February 2021). [12]

Jones, A., B. Sufrin and N. Dunne (2019), *Jones & Sufrin's EU Competition Law*, Oxford University Press. [6]

OECD (2024), *OECD Competition Trends 2024*, OECD Publishing, Paris, https://doi.org/10.1787/e69018f9-en. [8]

OECD (2023), *OECD Competition Trends 2023*, https://www.oecd.org/competition/oecd-competition-trends.htm. [32]

OECD (2023), *The Future of Effective Leniency Programmes: Advancing Detection and Deterrence of Cartels, OECD Competition Policy Roundtable Background Note*, https://www.oecd.org/daf/competition/the-future-of-effective-leniency-programmes-2023.pdf. [31]

OECD (2022), *OECD Peer Reviews of Competition Law and Policy: Tunisia*, https://www.oecd.org/daf/competition/oecd-peer-reviews-of-competition-law-and-policy-tunisia-2022.pdf. [1]

OECD (2021), *Competition Compliance Programmes, OECD Competition Policy Roundtable Background Note*, https://www.oecd.org/daf/competition/competition-compliance-programmes-2021.pdf. [42]

OECD (2021), *Recommendation of the Council on Transparency and Procedural Fairness in Competition Law Enforcement*, https://legalinstruments.oecd.org/en/instruments/OECD-LEGAL-0465. [4]

OECD (2020), *Criminalisation of cartels and bid rigging conspiracies: a focus on custodial, OECD Competition Policy Roundtable Background Note*, https://one.oecd.org/document/DAF/COMP/WP3(2020)1/en/pdf. [47]

OECD (2019), *Recommendation of the Council concerning Effective Action against Hard Core Cartels*, https://legalinstruments.oecd.org/en/instruments/OECD-LEGAL-0452. [33]

OECD (2018), *OECD Economic Surveys: Tunisia 2018*, OECD Publishing, https://doi.org/10.1787/eco_surveys-tun-2018-en. [9]

OECD (2016), *Sanctions in Antitrust Cases, OECD Competition Policy Roundtable Background Note*, https://one.oecd.org/document/DAF/COMP/GF(2016)6/en/pdf. [26]

OECD (2012), *Best Practice Principles for Regulatory Policy – The Governance of Regulators*, https://www.oecd.org/gov/regulatory-policy/governance-regulators.htm. [5]

OECD (2012), *Procedural Fairness and Transparency; Key Points*, OECD Publishing, https://www.oecd.org/daf/competition/mergers/50235955.pdf. [3]

OECD (2005), *Recommendation of the Council on Merger Review*, https://legalinstruments.oecd.org/en/instruments/OECD-LEGAL-0333. [11]

Philippine Competition Commission (2019), *Leniency Program - Frequently Asked Questions*, https://www.phcc.gov.ph/wp-content/uploads/2020/09/Leniency-Program-FAQs-09302020_final.pdf. [38]

Philippine Competition Commission (2018), *Merger Review Guidelines*, https://www.phcc.gov.ph/wp-content/uploads/2016/08/MERGER-REVIEW-GUIDELINE-October-092c-2018.pdf. [15]

Philippine Competition Commission (2018), *PCC Guidelines on Notification of Joint Ventures*, https://www.phcc.gov.ph/guidelines-on-notification-of-joint-ventures/. [24]

Statistiques Tunisie (2022), *Statistiques issues du répertoire national des entreprises*, http://www.ins.tn/sites/default/files/publication/pdf/RNE%202022.pdf. [10]

Ştefan, O. (2014), "Competition", *European Competition Soft Law in European Courts: A Matter of Hard Principles?*. [48]

Endnotes

[1] See for instance a comment from the US FTC on the recently published 2023 Merger Guidelines: *"The 2023 Merger Guidelines are a non-binding statement that provides transparency on aspects of the deliberations the Agencies undertake in individual cases under the antitrust laws. The Agencies will continue to make decisions in particular matters based on the law and the facts applicable to each case."* See also for instance the Consolidated Guidelines on Restrictive Trade Practices under the Competition Act by the Competition Authority of Kenya: *"These guidelines do not constitute legal advice, do not have the force of law, and is not binding on the Competition Tribunal or any court of law."*

[2] See for instance (Ştefan, 2014[48]): *"The ongoing research on which the present paper is based explores how the European Courts "take into account" non binding legally instruments such as the notices and the guidelines issued by the European Commission in the competition law sector. [...] During the last years the European Courts recognized legal effects and accepted article 241 objections of illegality of notices and guidelines, judged on matters such as their non-retroactivity and stated that under certain circumstances, soft law instruments are binding on the Commission."*

[3] See for instance (Banet, 2020[49]): *"If the guidelines are not de jure legally binding upon actors other than the Commission, the question remains of ascertaining whether they could be considered as de facto binding on the Member States due to their legal effects. Although case law makes clear that the Commission's guidelines are not legally binding upon Member States, the Court has also recognised that the guidelines could, under certain conditions and depending on their content, produce legal effects."*

[4] Case C-397/03 P, Archer Daniels Midland Co v. Commission [2006] ECR I-4429 at [91].

[5] This is supported by the comparative Table A A.2.

[6] The Commission is also unlikely to identify horizontal competition concerns in a merger with a post-merger HHI between 1 000 and 2 000 and a delta below 250, or a merger with a post-merger HHI above 2 000 and a delta below 150, except where special circumstances such as, for instance, one or more of the following factors are present: (a) a merger involves a potential entrant or a recent entrant with a small market share; (b) one of more merging parties are important innovators in ways not reflected in market shares; (c) there are significant cross-shareholdings among the market participants; (d) one of the merging firms is a maverick firm with a high likelihood of disrupting coordinated conduct; (e) indications of past or ongoing coordination, or facilitating practices, are present; (f) one of the merging parties has a pre-merger market share of 50 % of more (European Commission, 2008[21]).

[7] The Commission will not extensively investigate such mergers, except where special circumstances such as, for instance, one or more of the following factors are present: (a) a merger involves a company that is likely to expand significantly in the near future, e.g. because of a recent innovation; (b) there are significant cross-shareholdings or cross-directorships among the market participants; (c) one of the merging firms is a firm with a high likelihood of disrupting coordinated conduct; (d) indications of past or ongoing coordination, or facilitating practices, are present (European Commission, 2008[22]).

[8] As described in section 7.2, in Canada the existence of a compliance programme is treated as a mitigating factor, while in Belgium, the European Union and France a compliance programme is not considered as a mitigating circumstance for the purpose of setting fines.

[9] See (OECD, 2016[26]) for a more detailed assessment of mitigating and aggravating circumstances.

[10] It should be noted that only bid rigging is criminalised in Belgium, while the other selected jurisdictions criminalise hard core cartels in general (OECD, 2020[47]).

[11] For instance, the Canadian and Kenyan guidelines indicate 30 days, while the Philippine guidelines set 28 days (Competition Bureau, 2019, pp. 18, 33[39]; Competition Authority of Kenya, 2017, p. 7[37]). The European Commission Guidelines mention that in recent cases it has granted a one-month period, although this may be longer in certain cases (European Commission, 2022, p. 6[34]).

[12] According to (OECD, 2021, p. 16[42]), in 2012 France has adopted a policy to allow a fine reduction of up to 100% for the commitment to introduce or significantly improve an existing programme in the framework of the settlement procedure, on top of the 10% settlement reduction. However, a 2017 decision of the *Autorité de la concurrence* concluded that compliance programmes were expected to be incorporated by companies of a certain size and therefore they would not be considered as a mitigating factor when setting fines in cartel cases.

Annex A. Data on guidelines in selected jurisdictions

Table A A.1. List of merger guidelines for selected jurisdictions

Jurisdiction	Merger Guidelines	Date	Link
Selected OECD members			
Belgium	-	-	-
Canada	Merger Review Process Guidelines	2022	https://ised-isde.canada.ca/site/bureau-concurrence-canada/fr/comment-nous-favorisons-concurrence/education-sensibilisation/publications/lignes-directrices-concernant-processus-dexamen-fusions
	Procedures Guide for Notifiable Transactions and Advance Ruling Certificates Under the Competition Act	2022	https://ised-isde.canada.ca/site/bureau-concurrence-canada/fr/comment-nous-favorisons-concurrence/education-sensibilisation/publications/guide-procedure-legard-transactions-devant-faire-lobjet-dun-avis-certificats-decision-prealable-aux
	Hostile Transactions Interpretation Guidelines	2011	https://ised-isde.canada.ca/site/bureau-concurrence-canada/fr/avis-dinterpretation-transactions-hostiles
	Merger Enforcement Guidelines	2011	https://ised-isde.canada.ca/site/bureau-concurrence-canada/fr/comment-nous-favorisons-concurrence/education-sensibilisation/publications/fusions-lignes-directrices-pour-lapplication-loi
	Pre-Merger Notification Interpretation Guidelines	2011	https://ised-isde.canada.ca/site/bureau-concurrence-canada/fr/avis-dinterpretation-preavis-fusion-table-matieres
European Union	Commission Notice on a simplified treatment for certain concentrations under Council Regulation (EC) No 139/2004 on the control of concentrations between undertakings	2023	https://ec.europa.eu/transparency/documents-register/detail?ref=C(2023)2401&lang=en
	Commission Consolidated Jurisdictional Notice under Council Regulation (EC) No 139/2004 on the control of concentrations between undertakings	2008	https://eur-lex.europa.eu/legal-content/EN/TXT/?uri=CELEX%3A52008XC0416%2808%29
	Guidelines on the assessment of non-horizontal mergers under the Council Regulation on the control of concentrations between undertakings	2008	https://eur-lex.europa.eu/legal-content/EN/TXT/?uri=CELEX%3A52008XC1018%2803%29
	Commission Notice on Case Referral in respect of concentrations	2005	https://eur-lex.europa.eu/legal-content/EN/ALL/?uri=CELEX%3A52005XC0305%2801%29
	Commission Notice on restrictions directly related and necessary to concentrations	2005	https://eur-lex.europa.eu/legal-content/EN/TXT/PDF/?uri=CELEX:52005XC0305(02)&from=EN
	Guidelines on the assessment of horizontal mergers under the Council Regulation on the control of concentrations between undertakings	2004	https://eur-lex.europa.eu/legal-content/EN/ALL/?uri=celex%3A52004XC0205%2802%29
France	Merger review guidelines	2020	https://www.autoritedelaconcurrence.fr/sites/default/files/Lignesdirectricesconcentrations2020.pdf

Jurisdiction	Merger Guidelines	Date	Link
Selected non-OECD members			
Kenya	Joint Venture Guidelines	2021	https://cak.go.ke/sites/default/files/Competition_Authority_of_Kenya_Joint_Venture_Guidelines,_2021.pdf
	Consolidated Guidelines on the Substantive Assessment of Mergers under the Competition Act	Undated	https://cak.go.ke/sites/default/files/guidelines/Consolidated%20Merger%20Guidelines.pdf
Philippines	Revised Guidelines on Letters of Non-Coverage from Compulsory Notification	2019	https://phcc.gov.ph/guidelines-on-letters-of-non-notification-from-compulsory-notification/
	Guidelines on Notification of Joint Ventures	2018	https://phcc.gov.ph/guidelines-on-notification-of-joint-ventures/
	Merger Review Guidelines	2017	https://phcc.gov.ph/merger-review-guidelines-2/ (Online version is dated 2018)
	Guidelines on the Computation of Merger Notification Thresholds	Undated	https://phcc.gov.ph/guide-to-computing-merger-notification-thresholds/
South Africa	Guidelines on small merger notification – Revised small merger guideline.	2022	https://www.compcom.co.za/wp-content/uploads/2022/09/FINAL-GUIDELINES-ON-SMALL-MERGER-NOTIFICATION_.pdf
	Guidelines for the determination of administrative penalties for failure to notify mergers and implementation of mergers contrary to the Competition Act No 89 of 1998, as amended.	2019	https://www.compcom.co.za/wp-content/uploads/2020/04/42337_29-3_NationalGovernment-Compcom-Guidelines-FTN-and-PI.pdf
	Guidelines on the Assessment of Public Interest Provisions in Merger Regulation under the Competition Act No. 89 of 1998	2016	https://www.compcom.co.za/wp-content/uploads/2022/09/Guidelines-for-the-Assessment-of-Public-Interest-Provisions-in-Mergers.pdf

Note: Please note that this list has been confined to guidelines specifically focused on mergers. Other guidelines published by the competition authorities may also be relevant for the interpretation of the merger guidelines, for example, guidelines on market definition and guidelines on enforcement and remedies. Apart from Kenya, the Philippines and South Africa, the guidelines are not centrally located on the competition authorities' websites.

Table A A.2. Comparative table of merger guidelines in selected jurisdictions

Jurisdiction	Substantive test		Scope of guidelines			Market definition		Market structure and concentration			Competitive effects/market characteristics								Special provisions			
	Dominance	Restriction of competition	Horizontal	Vertical	Conglomerate	Product market	Geographic market	Market shares	Concentration ratio (e.g. CR4)	HHI	Unilateral effects	Coordinated effects	Barriers to entry/expansion	Buyer power	Import competition	Failing firm	Innovation effects	Efficiencies	Financial strength	*Safe harbours*	Public interest	Remedies
Selected OECD members																						
Belgium																						
Canada		✓	✓	✓	✓	✓	✓	✓	✓	✓	✓	✓	✓	✓	✓	✓	✓	✓		✓	✓	✓
European Union	✓	✓	✓	✓	✓	✓	✓	✓		✓	✓	✓	✓	✓		✓	✓	✓	✓	✓		✓
France	✓	✓	✓	✓	✓	✓	✓	✓		✓	✓	✓	✓	✓		✓	✓	✓		✓	✓	✓
Selected non-OECD members																						
Kenya	✓	✓	✓	✓	✓	✓	✓	✓	✓	✓	✓	✓	✓	✓	✓	✓	✓	✓			✓	✓
Philippines		✓	✓	*	*	✓	✓	✓		✓	✓	✓	✓	✓	✓	✓		✓	✓			✓
South Africa																					✓	

Note: This table is inspired by the comparative table of scope of merger guidelines prepared as part of the International Competition Network (ICN) Merger Working Group Project on Merger Guidelines, 2004, https://www.internationalcompetitionnetwork.org/wp-content/uploads/2018/05/MWG_MergerGuidelinesReport.pdf, p. 18. The table has been completed based only on the substantive merger guidelines in the selected jurisdictions.

Table A A.3. List of fining methodology guidelines for selected jurisdictions

Jurisdiction	Fining Methodology Guidelines	Date	Link
Selected OECD members			
Belgium	-*	-	-
Canada	-**	-	-
European Union	Guidelines on the method of setting fines imposed pursuant to Article 23(2)(a) of Regulation No 1/2003	2006	https://eur-lex.europa.eu/legal-content/EN/TXT/?uri=celex%3A52006XC0901%2801%29
France	Notice on the method for determining fines	2021	https://www.autoritedelaconcurrence.fr/sites/default/files/Communique_sanction.pdf
Selected non-OECD members			
Kenya	Competition Administrative Penalties and Settlement Guidelines	2020	https://cak.go.ke/sites/default/files/Competition%20Administrative%20Penalties%20and%20Settlement%20Guidelines.pdf
Philippines	-	-	-
South Africa	Guidelines for the Determination of Administrative Penalties for Prohibited Practices	2015	https://www.compcom.co.za/wp-content/uploads/2018/11/Final-Guidelines-for-Determination-of-Admin-Penalties-MAY-2015.pdf

Note: * Although Belgium has developed fining guidelines, they refer to the European Commission guidelines, only presenting specific adaptations to the Belgian context (available at https://www.belgiancompetition.be/sites/default/files/content/download/files/20200525_lignes_directrices_amendes_richtsnoeren_geldboeten.pdf). For this reason, they were not considered in the review carried out in this report.

** Canada does not have specific guidelines on fining methodology. However, the Abuse of Dominance Enforcement Guidelines from 2019 have a section on remedies, including on administrative monetary penalties (available at https://ised-isde.canada.ca/site/bureau-concurrence-canada/fr/comment-nous-favorisons-concurrence/education-sensibilisation/publications/lignes-directrices-labus-position-dominante). Given their limited scope, these guidelines were not considered in this report.

Table A A.4. List of leniency programme guidelines for selected jurisdictions

Jurisdiction	Leniency Programme Guidelines	Date	Link
Selected OECD members			
Belgium	Leniency Guidelines	2020	https://www.belgiancompetition.be/sites/default/files/content/download/files/20200522_clementierichtsnoeren_lignes_directrices_clemence.pdf
Canada	Immunity and Leniency Programs under the Competition Act	2019	https://ised-isde.canada.ca/site/bureau-concurrence-canada/fr/comment-nous-favorisons-concurrence/education-sensibilisation/programmes-dimmunite-clemence-vertu-loi-concurrence
European Union	Frequently Asked Questions (FAQs) on Leniency	2022	https://competition-policy.ec.europa.eu/system/files/2022-10/leniency_FAQs_2.pdf
France	Procedure Notice regarding the French leniency programme	2015	https://www.autoritedelaconcurrence.fr/sites/default/files/cpro_autorite_clemence_revise_0.pdf
Selected non-OECD members			
Kenya	Leniency Program Guidelines	2017	https://cak.go.ke/sites/default/files/guidelines/enforcement-compliance/Leniency%20Programme%20Guidelines.pdf
Philippines	Leniency Program Frequently Asked Questions	2019	https://www.phcc.gov.ph/wp-content/uploads/2020/09/Leniency-Program-FAQs-09302020_final.pdf
South Africa	Corporate Leniency Policy	2008	http://www.compcom.co.za/wp-content/uploads/2014/09/CLP-public-version-120520081.pdf

Note: *The Guidelines focus on horizontal mergers but note the underlying principles apply to vertical and conglomerate mergers. Separate guidelines on non-horizontal mergers will be prepared.

Table A A.5. List of compliance programme guidelines for selected jurisdictions

Jurisdiction	Compliance Programme Guidelines	Date	Link
Selected OECD members			
Belgium	Competition Rules – Guide for SMEs*	2016	https://www.abc-bma.be/sites/default/files/content/download/files/20160704_conformite_pme.pdf
Canada	Corporate Compliance Programs	2015	https://ised-isde.canada.ca/site/bureau-concurrence-canada/fr/comment-nous-favorisons-concurrence/conformite-application-loi/programmes-conformite-dentreprise
European Union	Compliance Matters	2012	https://op.europa.eu/en/publication-detail/-/publication/78f46c48-e03e-4c36-bbbe-aa08c2514d7a/language-en
France	Framework document of 23 May 2022 on competition compliance programmes	2022	https://www.autoritedelaconcurrence.fr/sites/default/files/2022-05/Conformite_nouveau%20doc-cadre%20ADLC.pdf
Selected non-OECD members			
Kenya	-	-	-
Philippines	-	-	-
South Africa	-	-	-

Note: * The Belgian Competition Authority has developed Guidelines on Competition Law to SMEs, which include a chapter on competition compliance programmes.

www.ingramcontent.com/pod-product-compliance
Lightning Source LLC
Chambersburg PA
CBHW061225240926
51846CB00006B/1353
9789264637740